RENEWED IN HIS PRESENCE

Satisfying Your Hunger for God

by
Lynne Hammond

Unless otherwise indicated, all Scripture quotations are taken from The Amplified Bible, The Old Testament copyright © 1965, 1987 by The Zondervan Corporation, Grand Rapids, Michigan. New Testament copyright © 1958, 1987 by The Lockman Foundation, La Habra, California. Used by permission.

Scripture quotations marked KJV are taken from the King James Version of the Bible.

Renewed in His Presence—
Satisfying Your Hunger for God

ISBN 1-57399-295-x
Copyright © 2001, 2005 by Lynne Hammond
Mac Hammond Ministries

Published by Mac Hammond Ministries
P.O. Box 29469
Minneapolis, MN 55429

Contents

Introduction	vii
1 God's Presence—Your Inheritance	1
2 Transformed to Do His Will	11
3 Faith and Fellowship: The Inseparable Connection	29
4 Choosing the "Good Portion"	53
5 Stay Hungry for God	75
6 Cultivating Holy Hunger	87
7 Walking With God	101
Prayer of Consecration	129

Introduction

A great move of God's Spirit has begun in the Church today. We are right on the edge of the greatest outpouring of the Holy Spirit mankind has ever known. This is a time for the people of God to seek Him with all their hearts like never before—not out of duty, but out of desire for the living God.

As for me, I can honestly say that I don't seek God out of a sense of duty, nor because I want to develop self-discipline. I seek Him because I love Him. The presence of almighty God fills my soul. I don't know how Jesus could become more dear or more near to me, and yet I'm so hungry for more of Him! I just want to know God in a deeper and more intimate way.

It's never been enough for me to just have God's power and glory in my life. I also want to be like Jesus. Whatever qualities Jesus possesses, that's what I want to possess. I want to be like Him in personality. I want to be like Him in character. When people see me, I want them to see Jesus.

To be like Jesus is my highest calling. It's the highest calling of every believer, because the only Jesus the world will ever see is the Jesus in us. We are His hands and His feet on this earth. We are His voice to the world. Therefore, we have to be transformed into His image so the world can see Him in us and be saved.

This has always been the emphasis of my life and ministry. But how about you? Do you sense a desire deep within your heart to experience more of the living God? Do you want His presence to become more real to you than your next breath? If so, then let this book help you cultivate that holy hunger for more of God. God's Spirit is moving, and you don't have to miss out on a single minute of it. You can discover how to be *Renewed in His Presence* every day of your life!

Lynne Hammond

Chapter 1

God's Presence— Your Inheritance

God longs to spend time in intimate communion with you. He wants to make Himself real to you. In fact, the very heart of the Gospel message is the truth that almighty God Himself waits, yearns, and eagerly desires for His redeemed children to come into His presence and fellowship with Him.

The presence of the Lord has always been the central fact of Christianity. I'm not just talking about His presence that dwells inside you because you're born again. I'm talking about the *manifest* presence of God!

You see, God never meant Christianity to merely be a set of rules and regulations. He never meant Christianity to be just an abstract theory or an impersonal doctrine. He doesn't want us to have a religion. He wants us to have a relationship with Him! He wants us to know Him personally. He wants us to experience His love so deeply that He becomes dearer to us than anything else in life.

The Greatest Treasure

In Psalm 84, we can read the words of an Old Testament saint who experienced the Lord in that way while worshiping in the tabernacle. Moved by the sweetness of God's manifest presence, he says:

> *How lovely are Your tabernacles, O Lord of hosts! My soul yearns, yes, even pines and is homesick for the courts of the Lord; my heart and my flesh cry out and sing for joy to the living God.*
>
> *Blessed (happy, fortunate, to be envied) are those who dwell in Your house and Your presence; they will be singing Your praises all the day long.*
>
> PSALM 84:1,2,4

What made the tabernacle so lovely to this person? God's manifest presence was there. In essence, the psalmist was saying, "There is little I need when I am in this place except God Himself. If everything else was stripped away—all my natural efforts, achievements, and possessions—and all I had was God, it would be enough. In God's tabernacle, I experience Him in a personal way. This isn't someone else's experience; I'm discovering Him for *myself*."

If you've ever experienced God's presence in that way, you know it's the greatest treasure you could ever have. But, like most Christians, you may have thought the treasure of God's manifest presence was hidden away, reserved for special occasions or "super saints." You may not have realized that you could experience that powerful presence every single day.

Jesus Promised to Reveal Himself

"Every day?" you ask. "How can I experience the presence of God every day? He doesn't always choose to reveal Himself that way!"

Yes, He does. The Bible says so.

You can see that for yourself in John 14. There we find one of the most important promises Jesus ever left with us. When Jesus gave this promise to His disciples, He was getting ready to leave His earthly ministry behind and enter into His high priestly ministry, sitting at the right hand of God. Jesus was letting His disciples know what would happen to them after He ascended to heaven.

At that time [when that day comes] you will know [for yourselves] that I am in My Father, and you [are] in Me, and I [am] in you.

The person who has My commands and keeps them is the one who [really] loves Me; and who-

> *ever [really] loves Me will be loved by My Father, and I [too] will love him and will show (reveal, manifest) Myself to him. [I will let Myself be clearly seen by him and make Myself real to him.]*
>
> JOHN 14:20,21

Remember, Jesus was speaking here to His disciples. We are also His disciples, so His words are for us as well. Jesus said, "I'm going to reveal Myself to you. I won't leave you floundering around in the dark. You're going to see Me clearly."

Jesus went on to say this in verse 23:

> *If a person [really] loves Me, he will keep My word [obey My teaching]; and My Father will love him, and We will come to him and make Our home (abode, special dwelling place) with him.*

So Jesus gives us this precious promise: "I'm going to leave and enter into My high priestly ministry, but you will still experience Me. You will still experience God the Father. You aren't going to live life just remembering how it used to be while acting as if you still have it today. Your Christianity won't be just a nice memory.

You don't have to settle for a "hearsay Christianity," where you hear someone else talk about his or her experience with God and say, "My, my! Isn't that nice! I wish that could happen to me." No, you can have a firsthand experience of your very own of His presence.

That is true Christianity. That's what each of us as believers should have in our relationship with God.

"I Know Him for Myself"

I hear people say, "I just can't find God." If *you* have ever felt that way, don't give up. Never stop seeking Him because He longs to manifest Himself to you personally.

God wants us to know Him for ourselves. That's exactly what John was talking about in 1 John 1:1-3:

> *[We are writing] about the Word of Life [in] Him Who existed from the beginning, Whom we have heard, Whom we have seen with our [own] eyes, Whom we have gazed upon [for ourselves] and have touched with our [own] hands.*
>
> *And the Life [an aspect of His being] was revealed (made manifest, demonstrated), and we saw [as eyewitnesses] and are testifying to and declare to you the Life, the eternal Life [in Him] Who already existed with the Father and Who [actually] was made visible (was revealed) to us [His followers].*
>
> *What we have seen and [ourselves] heard, we are also telling you, so that you too may realize and enjoy fellowship as partners and partakers with us. And [this] fellowship that we have [which is a distinguishing mark of Christians] is with the Father and with His Son Jesus Christ (the Messiah).*

Notice how careful John is to explain: "This is my own experience. I'm not telling you of someone else's experience. I've discovered Jesus for myself. I've seen Him. I'm an eyewitness of Him. I've heard Him. And I'm telling you all these things so you, too, can know Jesus. You can experience Him. You can fellowship with Him."

That is the essence of Christianity—the fact that we can each know, experience, and fellowship with God the Father and His Son, Jesus Christ, for ourselves. John says this fellowship we have with God is our *distinguishing mark*. In other words, every time we experience God's presence and sense Him moving in our hearts, it impacts our lives and leaves an impression of God on us that the rest of the world can see.

If you go through the Bible and read the accounts of all the great men and women of God, you'll find that the entire Book is an account of people's experience with the living God. Running throughout the Scripture is an invisible thread that constantly encourages us: "Seek God. Don't just mentally accept these words as true. Use them as a foundation for your faith, and then step into the experience of God which they point to: Seek to know the reality of God's presence in a personal way. Set out on a quest for Him. Wear out the path to Him. You don't have to just listen to others' experiences with God. You can discover Him for yourself."

Moses–Man of Destiny

Some believers don't realize how vital it is for them to experience the presence of God. They say,

"Oh, I have the written Word and that's enough for me."

But they're mistaken. It's not enough.

If you have a job to do, a divine assignment in the kingdom of God (and all of us do!), you need both the truth of God's Word and the presence of the Spirit to fulfill it.

You can look in the Bible and see that truth borne out in the lives of one great saint after another. Take Moses, for example. He had a great task set before him. In Exodus 33:1, the Lord instructed him:

> *Depart, go up from here, you and the people whom you have brought from the land of Egypt, to the land which I swore to Abraham, Isaac, and Jacob, saying, To your descendants I will give it.*

The Lord told Moses that He would send an angel before the Israelites to drive out the inhabitants of the land. Then He said, "But I will not go up among you, for you are a stiff-necked people, lest I destroy you on the way" (v. 3).

So Moses began to entreat the Lord:

> *See, You say to me, Bring up this people, but You have not let me know whom You will send with me.... Now therefore, I pray You, if I have found favor in Your sight, show me now Your way, that I may know You [progressively become more deeply and intimately acquainted with You, perceiving and recognizing and understanding more strongly and clearly].*

> *If Your Presence does not go with me, do not carry us up from here! For by what shall it be known that I and Your people have found favor in Your sight? Is it not in Your going with us so that we are distinguished, I and Your people, from all the other people upon the face of the earth?*
>
> EXODUS 33:12-13,15-16

Isn't that interesting? Moses lived under the old covenant, but he knew he had to have God's presence in a measure equal to the task that was before him.

In your life as a Christian, you also must have God's presence in a measure equal to His will, plan, and purpose for your life. That divine presence is what keeps you changing all the time so God can work His good pleasure in your life. (Philippians 2:13)

The Definition of Eternal Life

Just how important is it to know God in a personal and intimate way? Jesus revealed the answer in John 17:3 as He prayed to the Father by the unction of the Holy Spirit:

> *And this is eternal life: [it means] to know (to perceive, recognize, become acquainted with, and understand) You, the only true and real God, and [likewise] to know Him, Jesus [as the] Christ (the Anointed One, the Messiah), Whom You have sent.*

You know, a lot of people think that eternal life just means to exist forever. But that can't be true. Eternal life must mean far more than that because sinners are going to exist forever in a place reserved for the damned.

Well, then, is eternal life based on belonging to a particular church or religious group? No, Jesus tells us exactly what eternal life is in His prayer to the heavenly Father: *Eternal life is to know God and to know Jesus, the Messiah whom God has sent to us.*

You see, when we receive Jesus Christ as our Lord and Savior, we are guaranteed entrance into heaven when we die. But to fully enjoy eternal life, we must cultivate our relationship with God, progressively getting to know Him better.

Even Jesus had to maintain the life He had with the Father. There were times He had to depart to a mountain or a hillside and just be alone with God. And if Jesus had to do that, certainly we do as well. It is not just a matter of being born again or going to church once a week to get your spiritual "tank" filled up. Knowing God requires an ongoing fellowship with Him.

It's wonderful that so many people's lives have been touched by God. However, it's a sad story to me that not all Christians can say, "I have experienced Jesus for myself. I know Him. I have seen Him. I have heard Him. This fellowship I have is with the Father and His Son, Jesus Christ."

That should be your testimony. In fact, the only way you will ever be able to fulfill what God has called you to do, whatever that may be, is to know Him intimately and to walk moment by moment renewed in His presence.

Chapter 2

Transformed to Do His Will

I can tell you in three words why the manifest presence of God is so crucial to us right now. *It changes us.* And for us to become the glorious Church the New Testament tells about, fully transformed "unto the measure of the stature of the fullness of Christ" (Ephesians 4:13 KJV), we must be changed!

Sometimes when we look at where we are now, it's hard to imagine such a change is even possible. But we know it is because the Bible says that God:

> *...is able to do exceeding abundantly above all that we ask or think, according to the power that worketh in us, unto him be glory in the church*

> *by Christ Jesus throughout all ages, world without end. Amen.*
>
> EPHESIANS 3:20,21 KJV

The Bible promises us that we are going to be conformed to the image of Christ. (Romans 8:29) We are going to be more and more like Jesus. As we grow to be like Him, there will be such glory in the Church that the nations of the world will distinguish us from all the other peoples of the earth. (Deuteronomy 28:1; Jeremiah 33:9) God will glorify us in the midst of the nations. In fact, Isaiah 60:2–3 (KJV) says that so much glory will come forth from the Church, kings will come to our rising and our shining!

> *For, behold, the darkness shall cover the earth, and gross darkness the people: but the Lord shall arise upon thee, and his glory shall be seen upon thee. And the Gentiles shall come to thy light, and kings to the brightness of thy rising.*

This is our destiny as part of the body of Christ. God isn't looking at where we are right now. He's looking at where we are going to be. But for us to fulfill our glorious destiny, God has to change us by His Word and His presence.

Second Corinthians 3:17–18 (KJV) explains the process this way:

> *Now the Lord is that Spirit: and where the Spirit of the Lord is, there is liberty. But we all, with open face beholding as in a glass the glory of the Lord, are changed into the same*

image from glory to glory, even as by the Spirit of the Lord.

As we enter into God's glorious presence to behold Him, more glory comes, causing us to be transformed from one degree of glory to the next in an ever-increasing process of spiritual growth.

You see, in the kingdom of God, salvation and the baptism of the Holy Spirit are only introductory offers. The Lord is always offering us a higher degree of glory. But that greater glory can only be realized by allowing God's presence and His Word to change us.

How to Realize God's Perfect Will for You

As children of God, we are destined to be made in the image and likeness of Jesus. We are destined for glorification.

That's our ultimate destiny. But this process of transformation must take place before we can reach that destiny. Day by day, year by year, we must be changed by the presence of God.

Moses understood that principle. He knew that to carry out the task God had given him to fulfill, he had to be in a perpetual state of change. God's presence had to go with him every step of the way, or he'd never be able to do what he had to do.

Moses didn't need just the corporate presence of God, where people gather together to sing, dance, and praise the Lord. He needed to experience the power and presence of almighty God for himself. If he didn't have that, he knew he wouldn't make it.

God's presence and power are available to you in a way that is peculiar to your situation. God knows exactly how to change you and has tailor-made the way He manifests His presence to you in order to accomplish that change. His goal is to transform you from the inside out so you can accomplish His plan for your life.

Let me use my husband, Mac Hammond, as an example. Mac has been a minister for more than two decades now. But from the day Mac was born, it was always God's will that he preach the Gospel. However, for God's will to come to pass, Mac had to undergo a major change.

Mac became aware of God's call on his life to preach when he was twelve years old. As he sat listening to the preacher in a revival service in Charlotte, North Carolina, the presence of the Lord suddenly came down on him with tangible power.

That night and every night after that for a week, young Mac went down to the altar to weep and pray. His mother told me later, "Mac went to the altar and cried so much that I got embarrassed and told him not to go anymore!"

That wasn't the only time in Mac's life that God's presence came down on him in power. But it was this kind of experience that helped change him into the man of God he is today. God's presence was preparing

Mac for his call, growing him up so he could fulfill the divine plan and purpose for his life.

Now, Mac is just one example. Most of us have had our own experiences with the power of God's presence at one time or another. Why does God give us these life-changing experiences? He wants to change us from glory to glory into instruments He can use. He wants us to prove His perfect will for our lives.

The Burning-Bush Experience

Think again about Moses. Remember the experience he had with God out in the wilderness when he saw the burning bush? That remarkable encounter took place before Moses ever went into the land of Egypt to deliver his people from slavery.

Moses was walking through the wilderness, minding his own business. He probably wasn't even thinking about the presence of the Lord. But just then God came and met Moses there on that mountain, and His holy, manifested presence changed Moses forever.

God's presence made Moses resolute. It gave him purpose. It gave him both a plan and the knowledge that he could fulfill that plan because of the change God had wrought in him.

Before this burning-bush experience, Moses was in the same place we find ourselves in so much of the time. He'd gotten a glimpse of God's destiny for him years before. But after making some mistakes, he'd put God's plan on the shelf and settled into a life of tending sheep in the wilderness.

The same thing can happen to us. Every now and then as we're praying or worshiping God, we might get a glimpse of the plan God has for us. But some of us keep putting that plan on a back shelf. We keep shrinking back from it.

Or sometimes we don't have just a glimpse of the plan; we know *exactly* what God wants us to do. But we keep making excuses about why we aren't following His plan.

I remember one time, a businessman stopped to talk to me for a minute. He said, "You know, Sister Hammond, God wants me to do such-and-such with my businesses. But I don't know what all my business associates would think if I did that."

This man knew the will of God, but he wanted to obey God halfway. The other half of him wasn't sure if obedience was worth the cost.

He isn't an isolated case, either. Unfortunately, this is the testimony of too many Christians. God gives them a glimpse of His plan, but they decide they're just not ready to do all God wants them to do. They may want to cling to some things that hinder their Christian walk, such as relationships they know they should give up. So they shut God out because they don't want to hear what He has to say.

People in that kind of spiritual state may wander in the wilderness for a long time—until they have their own "burning-bush experience" where God's presence enters the scene to transform them and prepare them to fulfill His plan.

Saul: Changed by God's Presence

The book of 1 Samuel tells the story of Saul, another example of someone who was changed by the presence of God so he could be propelled into the plan of God. Here was a man who was going to be king. But Saul was a very timid, shy man. As he was, he couldn't stand in the position God had called him to fill. He wasn't ready to be a king.

If someone had said to Saul, "You're going to be king," he would have drawn back and said, "I can't be king. I don't have the means or the strength to be king." But God knew exactly how to make Saul ready. God placed him in a very strategic place where His presence could come and change Saul into the kind of man who could lead a nation.

First, Samuel came to anoint Saul as king of Israel. Then Samuel gave Saul some divine direction for his journey home:

> *After that you will come to the hill of God, where the garrison of the Philistines is; and when you come to the city, you will meet a company of prophets coming down from the high place with harp, tambourine, flute, and lyre before them, prophesying.*
>
> *Then the Spirit of the Lord will come upon you mightily, and you will show yourself to be a*

prophet with them; and you will be turned into another man.

1 SAMUEL 10:5,6

Notice what happened to Saul. Here was a man who couldn't fulfill his destiny in himself. He was actually an unspiritual man. So God sent Saul into a situation where His Spirit could come mightily upon him and prepare him for the task set before him as king of Israel.

If you've been trying to fulfill your destiny in your own strength, you may as well give it up. No one has ever been able to fulfill his divine destiny through his own efforts, and you can't do it either. The presence of God (and, of course, His Word) will have to change you to be what God wants you to be.

That's exactly what happened to Saul. God changed him into another man.

When these signs meet you, do whatever you find to be done, for God is with you.

And when [Saul] had turned his back to leave Samuel, God gave him another heart, and all these signs came to pass that day. When they came to the hill [Gibeah], behold, a band of prophets met him; and the Spirit of God came mightily upon him, and he spoke under divine inspiration among them.

1 SAMUEL 10:7,9,10

As Saul went on his way, he met that group of prophets. As Samuel had foretold, they were prophesying by the unction of the Holy Spirit. All Saul did was step into the manifest presence of the Lord that surrounded these prophets, and something began to happen to him.

Saul didn't decide on his own to speak as a prophet. But when he walked into the midst of God's manifested holy presence, that presence changed him so he could minister by inspired utterance.

And when all who knew Saul before saw that he spoke by inspiration among the [schooled] prophets, the people said one to another, What has come over [him, who is nobody but] the son of Kish? Is Saul also among the prophets?

1 Samuel 10:11

More and more in this day we live in, people are saying the same thing about a lot of believers who spend time in God's presence: "What's come over them? They almost seem like different people!" In a sense that's true, because these believers are in the process of being changed into the image of Jesus by the presence of almighty God.

But remember—it is God's presence on a daily basis that changes you. Every single day God wants to bring you to a new level in His presence that makes you equal to anything that is coming your way that day.

That's what happened to Saul. He was infused with such a strong presence of God that it made him equal to every challenge that had been set before him, including that of being Israel's king.

You see, when the manifested presence of God rushes into us and upon us, it makes us sufficient in Christ's sufficiency. God never intended for us to be at a loss for words. He never intended that a snare of the enemy would take us by surprise. We were not created to run around from crisis to crisis, putting out one fire after another in our lives. That was never God's plan. His plan was that we would be transformed by His presence to live in a perpetual state of preparedness, always equal to the task of fulfilling His good plan for our lives.

Don't Try to Change Yourself

Most of us want to fulfill God's perfect will for our lives, but that is only possible in proportion to our willingness to change.

We certainly can't fulfill God's plan by pushing and striving in our own strength, trying to do it all by ourselves. That never works. We can push and drive and strive all we want, but we'll come back to the same place every time where we have to admit defeat. (Just ask me how I know that!)

So if you've been trying to change yourself for years, just give up. You aren't going to do it on your own. You see, the habits, problems, and difficulties you need to change in your life are supernatural bondages that entered your life supernaturally. You aren't going to change supernatural bondage with natural strength. That type of bondage can only be changed by the power and presence of God.

Full of God's Presence—Full of His Will

One thing I've learned over the years is this: When you get full of God's presence, you get full of His will for your life. You'll never see a backslider full of the will of God.

Peter is a good example of what I'm talking about. Let's look first at how Peter reacted when Jesus was arrested and taken to the high priest for questioning.

> *But those who had seized Jesus took Him away to Caiaphas, the high priest, where the scribes and the elders had assembled. But Peter followed Him at a distance, as far as the courtyard of the high priest's home; he even went inside and sat with the guards to see the end.*
>
> MATTHEW 26:57,58

Fear and insecurity were already taking over Peter's emotions. He wasn't even a part of the crowd that was taking Jesus to the high priest. Peter's Master, the one who had taught him everything, was in trouble. Peter had been with Jesus constantly for three years. Yet now in the face of crisis, already he was shrinking back.

The temple guards took Jesus into the place where the elders and the Sanhedrin sat, waiting to question

Him. But Peter stopped and waited in the courtyard of the high priest's home.

From this point on, the plot worsens, as we well know. While Jesus was being accused and abused before the Sanhedrin, Peter stayed outside in the courtyard, denying that he even knew Him!

> *Now Peter was sitting outside in the courtyard, and one maid came up to him and said, You were also with Jesus the Galilean! But he denied it falsely before them all, saying, I do not know what you mean.*
>
> *And when he had gone out to the porch, another maid saw him, and she said to the bystanders, This fellow was with Jesus the Nazarene! And again he denied it and disowned Him with an oath, saying, I do not know the Man!*
>
> *After a little while, the bystanders came up and said to Peter, You certainly are one of them too, for even your accent betrays you. Then Peter began to invoke a curse on himself and to swear, I do not even know the Man!*
>
> *And at that moment a rooster crowed. And Peter remembered Jesus' words, when He had said, Before a single rooster crows, you will deny and disown Me three times. And he went outside and wept bitterly.*
>
> MATTHEW 26:69-75

This man, Peter, was always gripped by insecurity, fear, and timidity. But he could never have fulfilled the plan and will of God in the years to come with those characteristics. It was going to take great boldness to do what he was called to do. So somewhere along the way, Peter had to be changed.

That's exactly what happened. Something changed Peter from a fearful, timid man to a bold preacher of the Gospel of Jesus Christ. Acts 2 gives us the account of that "something":

> *And when the day of Pentecost had fully come, they were all assembled together in one place, when suddenly there came a sound from heaven like the rushing of a violent tempest blast, and it filled the whole house in which they were sitting. And there appeared to them tongues resembling fire, which were separated and distributed and which settled on each one of them.*
>
> ACTS 2:1-3

The manifested presence of God came down with power, settling as tongues of fire on the 120 who were gathered in that room. In an instant, every person present was changed forever.

> *And they were all filled (diffused throughout their souls) with the Holy Spirit and began to speak in other (different, foreign) languages (tongues)...*
>
> *Now there were then residing in Jerusalem Jews, devout and God-fearing men from every country under heaven. And when this sound was heard, the multitude came together.*
>
> ACTS 2:4-6

Notice that it says a *multitude* came together. Remember, we just read in Matthew 26 of a situation where Peter couldn't even speak the truth to one person. He couldn't even tell a little maid that he knew Jesus!

This multitude wanted to know what was going on. Verse 6 says, "They were astonished and bewildered, because each one heard them [the apostles] speaking in his own [particular] dialect."

Given Peter's past track record, you'd think he would have just turned tail and run from all those people. But look in verse 14 at how he responded to the situation: "But Peter, standing with the eleven, raised his voice and addressed them [the multitude]."

The first sermon Peter ever preached was to the multitudes! Personally, that impresses me because the first sermon I ever preached was to about ten people. I was so nervous, I could hardly breathe. My heart was beating so fast, I didn't know what was going to happen to me!

Yet Peter stood up and boldly addressed that multitude of people, saying, "You Jews and all you residents of Jerusalem, let this be [explained] to you so that you will know and understand; listen closely to what I have to say" (Acts 2:14).

I'm telling you, a great change had come over this man! The fountains of the deep that were on the inside of him had been broken up and released to flow out of him. Peter had been changed by the power of God. He got so filled up with God's presence that he became filled with the will of God. And he preached and preached and *preached* until three thousand were saved!

And don't forget—Peter wasn't the only one who came out of that room a changed person on the day of Pentecost. All the people who were there had had their own personal experience with God's presence—a supernatural experience that altered their personalities and put them in a yielded state so God could fulfill His will in their lives.

Saul of Tarsus: Changed by the Presence of God

Let's look at one more example of someone who was changed by the presence of God: Saul of Tarsus, later to be called Paul. Acts 9 describes Saul of Tarsus before God turned him around:

> Meanwhile Saul, still drawing his breath hard from threatening and murderous desire against the disciples of the Lord, went to the high priest and requested of him letters to the synagogues at Damascus [authorizing him], so that if he found any men or women belonging to the Way [of life as determined by faith in Jesus Christ], he might bring them bound [with chains] to Jerusalem.
>
> ACTS 9:1,2

This man had a real problem! All the time he was persecuting Christians, he thought he was doing God a wonderful favor! He knew the Scriptures well. Paul later said of himself that he was a Hebrew of Hebrews, trained in the Law as a Pharisee. (Philippians 3:5) And he was totally committed to wiping Christianity off the face of the earth.

But something happened to Paul on the road to Damascus one day.

> *Now as he traveled on, he came near to Damascus, and suddenly a light from heaven flashed around him, and he fell to the ground. Then he heard a voice saying to him, Saul, Saul, why are you persecuting Me [harassing, troubling, and molesting Me]?*
>
> *And Saul said, Who are you, Lord? And He said, I am Jesus, Whom you are persecuting.*
>
> ACTS 9:3-5

A light flashed out of heaven, brighter than the noonday sun. Saul was knocked off his horse. Then the manifest presence of God caused Saul to call Jesus *Lord!* That's amazing! Saul had never even called Him Savior yet!

God's presence was so great that it changed this man's name from Saul to Paul. And from that moment onward, he was ready to fulfill God's perfect will for his life.

Now, it was always God's will that Paul would write about one-half of the New Testament. It was always His will that Paul would be an apostle to the Gentiles. But Paul couldn't fulfill his destiny the way he was. He was breathing out threats and getting Christians killed throughout the region! He had to be changed by the presence of the Lord.

So it is with us, the Church of the Lord Jesus Christ. We are no different than Paul or any other man or woman of God in the Bible. It is God's presence that produces change in our hearts. In fact, one of the simplest revelations I have ever received from the Lord is that *we cannot produce change on our own.*

Time in His Presence

God has tailor-made experiences for you that are peculiar to your specific circumstances. They may not include a Damascus-road experience, but they are exactly what you need to get full of God's presence so you can fulfill His will for your life.

The Lord told me something many years ago that has stood the test of time. He said, *I can change anything about you. I can change your mind. I can change your personality. I can change your emotions. I can change your circumstances. I can change the way you feel about certain things. All you have to do is give Me one thing.*

I got excited when I heard that! I thought, *Surely I can give God one thing!* So I asked, "What is that one thing, Lord?"

Time in My presence, He replied.

Time is the one thing that none of us seem to have. But it is the one thing that God requires of us if we are to walk closely with Him.

You know, God is reasonable. Whatever He has called you to do, that divine call is in itself God's pledge to provide everything you need to stand in that place and to meet every single one of your responsibilities. If God requires something of you, just the requirement itself is His assurance that the means will be provided. That's an absolute guarantee you can base your faith on.

However, the foundation of your faith will always be in *knowing* God. And you will never know Him well unless you spend much time in His presence, allowing Him to transform you to do His will.

Chapter 3

Faith and Fellowship: The Inseparable Connection

One of the primary truths I have learned during my years of ministry is this: *Faith and fellowship with God are absolutely inseparable.* You cannot live by faith without maintaining a close fellowship with God.

The Bible says, "The just shall live by faith" (Romans 1:17 KJV). Since faith is the force that pleases God (Hebrews 11:6), one of your primary goals in life should be to develop strong faith.

The problem is, many Christians have become very mechanically minded about faith. They think, *If I follow these faith principles in my life—if I take step one and step* two and step three—*I'm going to reach step four and receive what I'm believing God for.*

But *principles* don't give you faith. The person of the Lord Jesus Christ is the source of your faith! Unless you know the giver of those faith principles, you will not go very far in your Christian walk.

Remember, Christianity is not just a set of principles we adhere to or a list of steps we take. Christianity is not even just a relationship with God. Rather, it is true fellowship and intimate communion with the Father and with His Son, Jesus Christ.

You probably already know that there is a great difference between *relationship* and *fellowship.* You don't suddenly know God just by becoming a Christian.

Think about the marriage relationship. Once a couple goes through a marriage ceremony, a legal contract has been established and the courthouse records show that they are husband and wife. But just because they have established that *relationship* doesn't mean they have any *fellowship.* They may live together for fifty years and never really get to know one another. I personally know many married couples who know absolutely nothing about enjoying fellowship or close communion with each other.

The same thing happens with many Christians in their relationships with the Lord. When they come to the altar to get saved, they shake hands with Jesus and say "hi." He responds, "Welcome to the family"—but that's as far as they allow their Christian walks to go.

My friend, that is *not* eternal life.

Do You Know Whom You Have Believed In?

So what does it mean when our relationship with God is void of fellowship? It means there is no joy, no real growth, and no faith in that relationship. The only way for us to walk in joy and faith is to become intimately acquainted with God.

Remember, Paul didn't say in 2 Timothy 1:12, "I know *what* I have believed." He said, "I know *whom* I have believed." The entire New Testament is all about developing a close communion with God. That's why Jesus died on the cross—to give us a way back to the Father. If we don't have that kind of intimate fellowship with God, we cannot serve Him with our whole heart.

I once heard someone say to another believer, "I know the Word of God."

The other person responded, "Yes, but do you know the God of the Word?"

I thought that was such a good answer. God doesn't want us to just know His principles or His steps to victorious living. Thank God for those principles and those steps! They are great teaching tools. But if we don't cultivate a close fellowship with God, His principles won't do us a bit of good.

That's why so many people are preaching faith and then falling by the wayside. You may know some of those people. They may have started out with you pursuing the things of God years ago. But now you look around and say, "Where are those people today?" They knew how to teach the principles, but they didn't maintain a close fellowship with God.

I don't want to fall by the wayside. My faith is not just in the Bible; my faith is in the person who wrote the Bible. I don't just love the Book because it's a book. I love that Book because I love Him!

The Ultimate Purpose of God's Word

Our desire to know God should be the driving force that motivates everything we do by faith. For instance, we pray in the name of Jesus all the time. But how often do we really seek to know the one who bears that name?

We shouldn't just love the *name* of Jesus; we should love the *person* of Jesus. With all our hearts, we should want to know Him and experience His presence in a greater measure. After all, that is the ultimate purpose of God's Word.

In John 5:38-40, Jesus made this complaint against the religious Jews, who didn't understand why God had given them the Scriptures in the first place:

You have not His word (His thought) living in your hearts, because you do not believe and adhere to and trust in and rely on Him Whom He has sent. [That is why you do not keep His message living in you, because you do not believe in the Messenger Whom He has sent.]

You search and investigate and pore over the Scriptures diligently, because you suppose and

> trust that you have eternal life through them.
> And these [very Scriptures] testify about Me!
> And still you are not willing [but refuse] to
> come to Me, so that you might have life.

Jesus was saying to those religious leaders, "You try to create for yourself an entire world by using My Word. But in that man-made world, you make Me and My presence unnecessary."

Those Jews revered the Scriptures, but they made the Scriptures an end in themselves. They didn't allow God's Word to reveal the one they desperately needed to receive as their Savior.

In essence, Jesus was telling them, "Not one of you has ever recognized what God is like. You have always been deaf to His voice and blind to the vision of His glory."

Those Pharisees were what you might call "Word people"—not according to the spirit of the Word, but according to the letter of the Law. They could outdo anyone in quoting the Old Testament. They poured over the Scriptures continually. They knew all *about* God, but they didn't *know* God.

How do we know that to be true? Because Jesus was manifesting God to these Pharisees right in their midst, and they didn't even recognize who He was! So Jesus told them, "You are not willing [but refuse] to come to Me, so that you might have life" (v. 40).

You can see that it is very possible to come to the Bible and yet not come to Jesus. It is possible to read the Bible and still not know the Lord. You can use a bunch of fancy, theological-sounding words, but that doesn't mean you have fellowship with God.

Knowing the God of the Word, Not Just the Word

Think about it—how many people do you know walking around in the world right now who can quote scriptures one right after the other, but they don't know Jesus? They may have the *letter* of the Word, but they don't live by the *Spirit* of the Word.

People can easily get off into spiritual error when they live only according to the letter of the Word. You see, a successful walk of faith requires the Word and the Spirit together. Believers need to receive both the impartation of the Holy Spirit and the Word of God preached from the pulpit or spoken personally to their hearts.

Jesus said to those Pharisees, "You search the Scriptures that you think you know so well, and they testify of Me. Yet you do not recognize Me, nor will you come to Me."

That's the way religion is. Religious people may seem very devout, but they don't project "Christ likeness," love, or compassion to those in need. For instance, when the man with the withered hand came to Jesus in the synagogue on the Sabbath day, those religious people were more interested in keeping their Sabbath day than they were in seeing the man get healed! (Matthew 12:10) They may have known the Old Testament Scriptures, but they didn't know the *Spirit* of the Scriptures.

So many Christians are like that. They want all the benefits of the new covenant without really knowing anything about the one who gave them that covenant.

One night when our church team was out on the streets talking to people about the Lord, I talked to several who fit that category. For instance, one man told me, "I've been saved, water baptized, and filled with the Holy Spirit. I've experienced it all! But I just wasn't able to live the Christian life."

I responded, "The reason you haven't been able to keep walking with God is that you haven't maintained the life of God on the inside of you. You haven't fellowshiped with God on a daily basis."

Many people make the same mistake this man did. They expect to meet the Savior—"Hi, Jesus, how are You?"—and then automatically live a victorious Christian life! But I'm telling you, those who are going to do something for God in these last days are those who want to really know Jesus for who He is.

I have kept one thing before me as a tremendous challenge ever since the day I was born again on September 5, 1972. I never wanted to be just a churchgoer or someone who knew the Scriptures. I wanted to become a person who was so filled and illuminated by the Spirit of God that others could see Christ in me.

That's what the Church of the Lord Jesus Christ needs now: to be filled to overflowing with God. Too often the world can't distinguish us from anyone else because we walk around looking like the world—no joy, no love, no life flowing out of us from the Spirit of God within. But that isn't what God intended. He wants us to be filled with the joy of deep, intimate, *wonderful* fellowship with Him.

Joshua and Caleb— Faith Born of Fellowship

Numbers 13 relates the account of the twelve men Moses sent to spy out the Promised Land. This account reveals a striking contrast in faith between those who were in fellowship with God and those who were not.

Before this time, the word of the Lord had come to the Israelites again and again, telling them, "This is the land I have given to you. It is a land flowing with milk and honey." All the leaders heard those words, as did all the children of Israel. Yet there were two men who heard those words differently than the rest.

As we look at the account in Numbers 13, you'll see what I mean.

> *And the Lord said to Moses, Send men to explore and scout out [for yourselves] the land of Canaan, which I give to the Israelites. From each tribe of their fathers you shall send a man, every one a leader or head among them.*
>
> *So Moses by the command of the Lord sent scouts from the Wilderness of Paran, all of them men who were heads of the Israelites.*
>
> NUMBERS 13:1-3

Verses 4-15 then go on to list the names of the tribal leaders that Moses sent out. Now, surely the heads of Israel's tribes would have the Word of God in their hearts! Certainly God expected them to believe and act on what He had already told them about the land.

Let's read on to see what Moses told the spies to do when they entered the Promised Land.

> *Moses sent them to scout out the land of Canaan, and said to them, Get up this way by the South (the Negeb) and go up into the hill country, and see what the land is and whether the people who dwell there are strong or weak, few or many, and whether the land they live in is good or bad, and whether the cities they dwell in are camps or strongholds, and what the land is, whether it is fat or lean, whether there is timber on it or not. And be of good courage and bring some of the fruit of the land. Now the time was the time of the first ripe grapes.*
>
> NUMBERS 13:17-20

So the twelve spies followed Moses' instructions. Verse 23 says that "they came to the Valley of Eshcol, and cut down from there a branch with one cluster of grapes, and they carried it on a pole between two [of them]." Just imagine how big that cluster of grapes must have been if two men had to carry it on a pole laid across their shoulders! This really *was* a land "flowing with milk and honey"!

In verses 25-26, we learn about the twelve spies' return:

> *And they returned from scouting out the land after forty days. They came to Moses and Aaron and to all the Israelite congregation in the Wilderness of Paran at Kadesh, and brought them word, and showed them the land's fruit.*

Verse 26 says the spies "brought them word." Notice, however, that the word the spies brought the children of Israel wasn't *the* Word that God had spoken to them; it was just *a* word, and not a very good word at that! Look at what the spies said:

> *We came to the land to which you sent us; surely it flows with milk and honey. This is its fruit. But the people who dwell there are strong, and the cites are fortified and very large; moreover, there we saw the sons of Anak [of great stature and courage].*
>
> *Amalek dwells in the land of the South (the Negeb); the Hittite, the Jebusite, and the Amorite dwell in the hill country; and the Canaanite dwells by the sea and along by the side of the Jordan [River].*
>
> NUMBERS 13:27-29

These spies knew all about their enemies. They could describe what each tribe looked like and where they all lived. However, they didn't seem to know too much about God's promise to give them the land within which their enemies dwelt!

But we find out in Numbers 13:30 and 14:6 that the twelve spies were not unanimous in their doubt and unbelief. Joshua and Caleb, two of the leaders sent to scout out the land, had something very different to say about the land God had promised the children of Israel.

Look at what Caleb said in verse 30:

> Caleb quieted the people before Moses, and said, Let us go up at once and possess it; we are well able to conquer it.
>
> NUMBERS 13:30

Caleb's response to what he and the others had seen was strikingly different from the first report. All twelve men started out with the same potential. They were all leaders appointed by God. They had all heard the same words. They had all been given the same opportunity to believe God's promise to them.

But ten of the men failed the test of leadership. They heard God's Word and refused to believe it. They gave an evil report of doubt and unbelief: "We are not able to go up against the people [of Canaan], for they are stronger than we are" (v. 31).

The ten spies continued with their evil report in verses 32-33:

> The land through which we went to spy it out is a land that devours its inhabitants. And all the people that we saw in it are men of great stature. There we saw the Nephilim [or giants], the sons of Anak, who come from the giants; and we were in our own sight as grasshoppers, and so we were in their sight.

Joshua and Caleb did all they could to convince the people not to listen to the words of unbelief coming from their fellow scouts. In Numbers 14:7-9, the two men said to the Israelites:

> *The land through which we passed as scouts is an exceedingly good land. If the Lord delights in us, then He will bring us into this land and give it to us, a land flowing with milk and honey.*
>
> *Only do not rebel against the Lord, neither fear the people of the land, for they are bread for us.*

"Stop rebelling against God!" Joshua and Caleb pleaded with the people. How did the people rebel against the Lord? *By not believing what God had said to them.*

The truth is, anything less than having faith in the words God has spoken is rebellion against Him. Personally, I choose to believe the Word of God. I'm not going to be a rebel!

The Israelites weren't inclined to listen to Joshua and Caleb's good report. In fact, verse 10 says, "All the congregation said to stone [Joshua and Caleb] with stones."

Judgment was about to fall on the Israelites for their hardheartedness in the face of God's promise. Then Moses interceded before the Lord on behalf of His people:

> *Pardon, I pray You, the iniquity of this people according to the greatness of Your mercy and lov-*

ing-kindness, just as You have forgiven [them] from Egypt until now.

And the Lord said, I have pardoned according to your word.

NUMBERS 14:19,20

Notice that God said to Moses, "I'll pardon the people according to *your* word, Moses—because of what you have said in your intercession for them." This shows us the close relationship God had with Moses, developed from extended times of intimate fellowship.

Although the people were spared from destruction through Moses' intercession, they still faced consequences for their doubt and unbelief. In Numbers 14:22-24, God talks about those consequences. He also contrasts Caleb with the rest of the Israelites:

Because all those men who have seen My glory and My [miraculous] signs which I performed in Egypt and in the wilderness, yet have tested and proved Me these ten times and have not heeded My voice, Surely they shall not see the land which I swore to give to their fathers; nor shall any who provoked (spurned, despised) Me see it.

But My servant Caleb, because he has a different spirit and has followed Me fully, I will bring into the land into which he went, and his descendents shall possess it.

Later on in verse 30, God includes Joshua in this select group of the faithful who would enter the

Promised Land: "Surely none shall come into the land in which I swore to make you dwell, except Caleb son of Jephunneh and Joshua son of Nun."

Joshua and Caleb were the only two who, after hearing the Word, stood on God's promise in the midst of heavy opposition.

As I read this account, I thought, *There must be a good reason why Joshua and Caleb stayed strong in faith when the crowd chose to act in doubt and unbelief.* Then the Lord prompted me to read Exodus 33 and I saw what that reason was. I saw that while Moses prayed in the tent of meeting, Joshua stayed right there with him.

> *When Moses entered the tent, the pillar of cloud would descend and stand at the door of the tent, and the Lord would talk with Moses.*
>
> *And the Lord spoke to Moses face to face, as a man speaks to his friend. Moses returned to the camp, but his minister Joshua son of Nun, a young man, did not depart from the [temporary prayer] tent.*
>
> Exodus 33:9,11

This passage of Scripture reveals something about Joshua. His heart's desire was to linger in the place of God's manifest presence! During those times spent in the tent of meeting, Joshua had developed an intimate fellowship with God, just like his mentor, Moses.

That fellowship kept Joshua's faith very strong. The same was true for Caleb. In Joshua 14, Caleb laid claim to his inheritance within the Promised Land. As he pled his case before Joshua, Caleb talked about what had happened forty years earlier when the twelve spies returned from scouting out the land:

> Forty years old was I when Moses the servant of the Lord sent me from Kadesh-barnea to scout out the land. And I brought him a report as it was in my heart. But my brethren who went up with me made the hearts of the people melt; yet I wholly followed the Lord my God.
>
> JOSHUA 14:7,8

In other words, Caleb had such intense fellowship with God that he could do nothing except what was in his heart, no matter what circumstances he faced. It was because of that close fellowship with the Lord that Caleb's heart said, "God has given me this land; therefore, it's mine to claim!"

Verses 13,14 tell us the result of Caleb's wholehearted fellowship with God:

> Then Joshua blessed him and gave Hebron to Caleb son of Jephunneh for an inheritance. So Hebron became the inheritance of Caleb son of Jephunneh the Kenizzite to this day, because he wholly followed the Lord, the God of Israel.

The example of Joshua and Caleb shows you that whatever is most magnified in your heart is what you will follow. If oppression is the thing most magnified in your heart, then oppression is what you will follow.

On the other hand, if your "promised land" of healing, peace, direction, prosperity, and joy is magnified in your heart, no one will be able to steal those blessings away from you. It won't matter what the Devil tries to bring your way, you will walk in your "promised land," enjoying the covenant benefits God has provided for you through Jesus.

However, the only way those covenant blessings can be magnified in your heart is through fellowship with God. You have to get alone with Him, earnestly seeking His face and letting Him minister to you.

Discovering Hidden Treasure Through Fellowship

One way God ministers to you in those quiet times alone with Him is to give you guidance and direction. For instance, someone may give you a legitimate "word from the Lord" about God's plan for your life. However, that word isn't going to stay in your heart if you only hear it from someone else. You need God to speak to you about it on a personal basis as you spend time alone with Him.

God may speak to you from His Word, or He may speak to your heart in a time of fellowship and prayer. But once you know you have heard from God for yourself, no one will be able to shake what He has said from your heart!

One time, a very busy minister's wife came to my church office desiring to pray with me. We talked for a while before we prayed, and we both came to a profound but simple conclusion: She and her husband greatly needed God's direction in their lives and ministry.

So I talked to this woman about her need to spend time alone with God, seeking direction and guidance. She got out her little daily planner to find a time she could regularly put aside for God. But as she looked at her packed schedule, she began to talk herself out of it.

"Let me see now," she said. "On Monday I don't have any extra time at all. Tuesday is full too. Let's see about Wednesday...."

As I listened, I wanted to say to this woman, "You're treating this matter of spending time with God as if it were optional, and it isn't at all!"

Many Christians have come to that point in their Christian walks. Spending time with the heavenly Father—the very source of their life, joy, guidance, direction, and strength—has become optional in their lives. They actually have to be convinced that this most basic, bottom-line aspect of the Christian walk is an absolute requirement in order to enjoy God's covenant blessings in this life.

So I began to do what I could to convince this minister's wife of this fact. I said, "Now, Sister, wait a minute. We have both clearly seen by the Holy Spirit today that you and your husband have to receive divine direction for your lives. But how are you going to receive that direction if you don't draw near to God and seek His face?"

I'll tell you how a lot of people try to get it. They call their neighbor on the telephone, or they call the church and want someone to prophesy to them and tell them what to do!

However, God doesn't work like that. The truth is, if you don't know what God wants you to do in a particular situation, you haven't spent enough time with Him. First, you need to spend more time reading the Word. Second, you need to seek the face of God in prayer.

Just think for a moment about where diamonds, rubies, and sapphires are found. They don't lie scattered on top of the ground where anyone can casually pick them up and do whatever they want with them. These precious stones lie hidden deep within the earth. Anyone who wants to find them has to be willing to spend a lot of time and effort preparing to dig for them.

It's the same way in the spiritual realm. The wisdom and direction you need, the gifts God has given you—all these things are hidden deep down on the inside of you like precious treasures waiting to be discovered. But you have to be ready to receive these treasures. How do you get ready? Through daily times of intimate fellowship with God.

Learning to Hear When God Speaks

I've had many people say to me, "I'm having trouble hearing the voice of God. How can I learn to hear His voice?"

Maybe you've asked the same thing yourself, so let me answer that question with an illustration. Suppose

Faith and Fellowship: The Inseparable Connection

you and I are standing on opposite sides of a large auditorium and I want to talk to you. I try to yell across the room, but you can't quite hear me. What could you do to hear me better? You could move closer to where I am standing!

Well, that's what you need to do in your relationship with God. You need to draw much, much closer to Him than you are right now. You need to become so well acquainted with Him that you recognize His gentle, small voice in your spirit the moment He speaks.

Consider how easy it is to discern your mother's voice in a crowd. Why is that? Because you lived with your mother for years. You have heard her speak when she was sad, when she was glad, and when she was mad. You heard her speak in the morning, at noontime, and at night. You have heard her full range of expression for many years. Because you know your mother so well, you would know her voice anywhere.

It's the same way in your relationship with God. If you want to know His voice when He speaks to you, you will have to spend much time fellowshiping with Him.

I once heard a brother in the Lord testify about a time he heard from God. For a long time, he had been praying, "Lord, I want to hear You. I want to do Your will. God, please talk to me!"

This man wanted God to talk to him in his mind. But God is a Spirit, so He doesn't speak to His people in their minds; He speaks to them in their *spirits*.

Finally, this man got quiet enough to hear the Holy Spirit's gentle voice in his spirit. These are the words the man heard: *I'll talk to you from the Book.*

This is God's message to you as well. Reading the Bible is the very first key to fellowship because God wants to speak to you from His Word. But it takes *time* to read the Word, and time is the primary thing the Devil wants to steal from you.

You see, time is the most precious thing you have. It is certainly much more precious than money or possessions. If material things are lost, they can be replaced. But once you lose time, it is gone forever.

The Devil is out to make his play in your life. He knows if he can rob you of time, he can cut into your faith. If he can cut into your faith, he can cut into your quickness to obey God and begin to steal the will of God for your life.

Now you can see why spending time with God isn't optional. It's vital! And the first thing you must do is to spend time reading His Word.

You shouldn't read the Bible just to accumulate information, however. First Corinthians 8:1 warns you that knowledge in itself will puff you up. Only when knowledge is gained through loving communion with God will it edify and bless your walk with Him. So read your Bible *prayerfully, with your spirit alert, constantly expecting God to speak to you through His written Word.*

The second thing you need to do to develop a sensitivity to God's voice is to increase your prayer life. It's actually very simple; the only way to develop intimacy with God is to read the Bible and pray. These are bottom-line, basic keys that cannot be ignored.

So think about it for a moment. How much time do you take to pray every day? How much time do you spend fellowshiping with God in His Word? God wants you to talk to Him, and He wants you to recognize His voice when He talks back to you.

But let me give you a word of caution here. Don't allow yourself to get in the habit of what I call "phony fellowship." That's when you go into your prayer closet and let your mind bounce from one subject to the next as your mouth prays to God.

You aren't even that rude to the people you talk to throughout the day! When you hold a conversation with another person, both of you concentrate on what you are saying to each other.

That's what you need to do with the Lord. One of the most important aspects of communing with God in prayer is learning to keep your mind centered on Him. This kind of focused attention is absolutely required if you are ever going to learn to discern His voice.

Walking in the Manifest Presence of God

Another crucial aspect of prayer is to learn how to enter His presence through praise and worship.

Let me tell you something—God isn't the frivolous character we sometimes think He is.

God is an awesome being. He is holy and pure. So as we come before God's throne in praise and worship, there will be times when all we can do is lie prostrate before Him in the majesty of His manifest presence.

You see, the presence of God and the manifest presence of God are not the same. The presence of God is always there. But when God *manifests* Himself to you, you become tangibly aware of His presence.

Walking in the manifest presence of God is the difference between your living a nominal Christian life and a life filled with the fire of the Holy Ghost.

"But Lynne," you might say, "what if I spend hours seeking and yearning after God and I still don't find Him?" Don't worry about that. God wants to manifest Himself to you. He wants you to know Him better. In fact, He promised in Hebrews 11:6 that He is the rewarder of those who diligently seek Him. And you can rest assured He will keep that promise.

So you can pray in faith for increasing degrees of awareness and a more perfect consciousness of God. You can pray like the apostle Paul did, "that the God of our Lord Jesus Christ, the Father of glory, may give unto you the spirit of wisdom and revelation in the knowledge of him: the eyes of your understanding being enlightened..." (Ephesians 1:17,18 KJV).

You can also ask the Holy Spirit, who dwells within you every moment of every day, to help you become more sensitive to His guidance. As you spend time fellowshiping with the Lord on a daily basis, you will find your prayers being answered beyond anything you could have imagined. You will learn to recognize God's voice the moment He speaks to your heart. And your faith will grow ever stronger as you walk in His presence each day!

Chapter 4

Choosing the "Good Portion"

It's time to get honest with yourself. Are you just going to pretend that you're walking with God, or are you really going to walk with Him? God has laid that choice squarely in your hands.

You might say, "Well, I was intending to get up this morning and pray" or "I don't know how I started going the wrong direction because I intended to do it God's way."

But God doesn't bless your good intentions. He blesses your obedience to what He tells you as you fellowship with Him in the Word and in prayer. It is only through close fellowship with God that you receive the answers you need from Him to grow up spiritually and walk in His covenant benefits.

You see, fellowship is a progressive process. It is difficult to fellowship with a baby, both in the natural and in the spiritual realm. That's why God wants us to grow up; He wants to fellowship with us on His higher level of thinking. As Isaiah 55:9 (KJV) says, "For as the heavens are higher than the earth, so are my ways higher than your ways, and my thoughts than your thoughts."

Do you know why our thoughts are not as high as God's thoughts? Because we don't spend enough time with Him to get to know Him!

The Bible says that in the last days, "the people that do know their God shall be strong, and do exploits" (Daniel 11:32 KJV). Notice that those who are strong and do exploits for God are *not* those who can quote scriptures, but those who have grown up enough spiritually to *know* their God.

Regulating Your Life in Conformity to God

Colossians 2:6 gives us a clear guideline to follow in order to reach that higher level of fellowship with God:

> *As you have therefore received Christ, [even] Jesus the Lord, [so] walk (regulate your lives and conduct yourselves) in union with and conformity to Him.*

Once you have received Jesus as your Savior, you are to regulate and conduct your life *in union with and in conformity to God*. Of course, you were made one with the Lord when you were born again. (1 Corinthians 6:17) But to live each day in union with God, you must choose to regulate your life around your highest priority—time spent in fellowship with Him.

Notice what verse 7 goes on to say:

Have the roots [of your being] firmly and deeply planted [in Him, fixed and founded in Him], being continually built up in Him, becoming increasingly more confirmed and established in the faith, just as you were taught, and abounding and overflowing in it with thanksgiving.

As you regulate your life and conduct yourself in conformity to Jesus, you constantly become more rooted, more grounded, and more established in God's Word and in His power.

What does it mean to be rooted in God? It means you are always increasing, always growing. You are stalwart and steadfast. You are becoming more like Jesus every day. It is becoming more and more difficult for you to be dismayed, discouraged, or defeated. You find yourself becoming less and less distracted from the things of God.

But to reach this place in your spiritual walk, you have to regulate your life in fellowship and in union with God. And understand this: You are the one who does the regulating, just as you use a thermostat to regulate the temperature in your home. If it gets cold at night, you turn on the heat. If it gets hot during the day, you turn on the air conditioner.

So it is with your spiritual life. In order to keep growing in God, you must constantly check your "spiritual temperature" and then regulate your fellowship with Him accordingly.

Living in Perpetual Deliverance

I can't count the times I have told people who come to me for prayer or counseling, "You need to spend more time with God." So often these same people never receive their deliverance because they allow themselves to remain trapped in the business of life.

However, I remember one woman who did receive her deliverance. When I first saw her, my heart went out to her because she always walked into church with her head down, looking so unhappy.

So I prayed, "Lord, I know this woman needs more of You. If there is anything I can do, I'd like to help her. Show me how to talk to her without scaring her off."

Not long after praying that prayer, I went over to this woman after the Sunday morning service. I took her hand and casually said, "If you ever want to talk to me, I'm available."

The very next week, the woman called me and said, "I'd like to come in and talk to you."

Choosing the "Good Portion"

When she came in, I started asking a few questions to get to know her a little better. She began to cry as she told me the horrible story of her life.

As this woman talked to me, I could see why she always seemed so sad and insecure. Her life had been a tangled mess from the time she was born to the present. As I listened to her awful story, I began to weep with her.

As I sat there crying, I thought, *Now, this is no good! I was going to be a help to this woman, not a hindrance! But, Lord, I don't have an answer for any of this. Please show me what to do.*

Immediately the Lord spoke to my heart. *Just get her to My throne,* He said.

Well, I can do that! I thought.

So after the woman finished talking, I said to her, "Let's pray. I want you to tell the Lord everything you just told me."

So she did. Both of us cried as she talked to the Father for a long, long time, pouring out her heart before Him. But by the time this woman was finished, God had mightily delivered her! She was so filled with joy and her deliverance was so marvelous that no human being could take any credit for it. We were just consumed with God's presence, and in that glorious presence, this woman was completely set free by the mighty hand of God.

Today this woman is in a position of church leadership. She walks with her head held high and is a dynamic powerhouse for God. At one point she told me, "You know, deliverance is wonderful, and I so appreciate what the Lord did for me that day. *But the greatest thing He has ever done for me is keep me in perpetual deliverance through my fellowship with Him.*"

This is exactly where most Christians miss it. God gloriously sets them free from sin, bad habits, sickness, and so forth. But because they don't maintain that deliverance through regular fellowship with God, they allow themselves to slip back into bondage.

My friend, God isn't just your deliverer for today. God is a deliverer to you every single day of your life! The Bible says that He *has* delivered you! (Colossians 1:13) From now throughout eternity, God *has* delivered and He *will continue* to deliver you.

You may think of Jesus as your one-time Savior who saved you on the day you were born again. But Jesus is your Savior every day! He saves you out of the biggest messes! He has miracles for you every day, if you will only believe in Him and depend on Him for your salvation and deliverance in every situation of life.

The "Good Portion": Sitting at the Feet of Jesus

Luke 10:38-42 tells about two sisters named Mary and Martha. Mary reminds me of this woman I just told you about who stays in perpetual deliverance through fellowship with God. The other woman,

Martha, reminds me of the many Christians who have gotten trapped in the busyness of life.

> Now while they were on their way, it occurred that Jesus entered a certain village, and a woman named Martha received and welcomed Him into her home. And she had a sister named Mary, who seated herself at the Lord's feet and was listening to His teaching.
>
> But Martha [overly occupied and too busy] was distracted with much serving; and she came up to Him and said, Lord, is it nothing to You that my sister has left me to serve alone? Tell her then to help me [to lend a hand and do her part along with me]!

You know, this account could have been left out of the Bible. It doesn't tell us about one of Jesus' great miracles, such as healing a blind man or causing the lame to walk again. This story is just about a time when Jesus visited someone's house. It could have been left out of the Bible so easily, but it wasn't.

I believe God had a very good reason for including this passage of Scripture. In one sense, it is a prophetic message for the Church in these last days.

Notice that both of these women were given the same opportunity to increase and advance in God through Jesus' visit to their home. Both of them loved Jesus. Both of them wanted to serve Jesus with all their hearts. But Mary chose a different way than her sister did to demonstrate her love for the Master.

Verse 39 says Mary *seated herself* at the feet of Jesus. No one said, "Come on over here, Mary, and sit down. Jesus is going to preach now." On the contrary, Martha was hollering at her to come and help in the kitchen!

So many voices bombard us, distracting us each day from spending time with God. "Will you help me do this? Can you come to my house? Let's do this today."

Martha's voice was pressuring Mary to get up and help with dinner preparations. Nevertheless, Mary *seated herself*. That means she made a quality decision. She probably thought, *I'm going to sit down here, come hell or high water, and listen to my Jesus!* Mary was following the scriptural principle that says *the violent take the kingdom of God by force*. (Matthew 11:12)

You have to do the same thing with your fellowship with God. Take it by force! You're not going to get quality time with God by saying, "What will be, will be. Maybe I'll find some time to spend with God; maybe I won't."

You'll never develop a close relationship with God with that kind of attitude! The things of God will cost you something. There is a price to be paid for His treasures. You won't discover them in the shallowness and busyness of everyday life.

Let's look again at what Martha said to Jesus regarding Mary's decision to seat herself at His feet: "Lord, is it nothing to You that my sister has left me to serve alone? Tell her then to help me [to lend a hand and do her part along with me]!"

Now, that's pressure! It's the same way in your own life. You'll sense pressure coming from a lot of different directions whenever you want to sit down and be with God.

"What is Mary doing, Jesus?" Martha complained. "How absurd! Look at her! Here I am, doing all the work, and she is sitting there listening to You! Who does she think she is? Jesus, tell Mary to lend a hand and do her part to help me!"

Jesus' response to Martha's complaint was unexpected and profound, and it absolutely applies to each of our lives in these last days:

> But the Lord replied to her by saying, Martha, Martha, you are anxious and troubled about many things; there is need of only one or but a few things. Mary has chosen the good portion [that which is to her advantage], which shall not be taken away from her.
>
> LUKE 10:41,42

"There is need of only one thing," Jesus said, "and I am calling you to do this one thing as well. Mary has chosen the good portion, and it is to her advantage."

Sitting there with Mary at His feet, Jesus said to Martha, "Your sister is getting the advantage on you!" That certainly isn't the way the world thinks!

According to the world's way of thinking, Martha made the right decision and Mary made the wrong one. The world would say, "Mary, you are lazy. You aren't doing your part. Get up and work!"

But Jesus didn't say that. He said, "Mary has chosen the good portion, and it won't be taken away from her."

Martha was a wonderful person, but her life had become so complicated that she couldn't obey or receive from Jesus. She had overcrowded her life with too many things. Those things were not sinful; they were good, commendable, legitimate interests and activities. But they had cluttered Martha's life so much that they finally distracted her from enjoying *the good portion*—spending quality time with Jesus.

Too many Christians make the same mistake Martha did. They get caught up with activities and interests that are good and commendable in themselves. However, these things lack the substance and wisdom needed to move higher in God. Only in communion with Jesus can that eternal substance be found.

Don't Miss Those Special Moments With God

What if you heard that Jesus was coming to your town and had chosen to visit your home while He was there? What would your reaction be?

Would you be wise like Mary and say, "You know, I'm going to hire a caterer and just sit at Jesus' feet while He's here"? Or would you be a "Martha" and spend Jesus' entire visit in the kitchen being busy and bothered with all the practical details?

You know, Jesus' visit to Mary and Martha's home was probably a short one—no more than a few hours. It was up to the two women to make the most of their opportunity during the short time Jesus was in their midst.

In the same way, Jesus will give you special moments throughout your life—times when He expects you to settle down and get rid of all distractions so He can manifest His presence to you. And just as the children of Israel ate fresh manna every day, God delights in giving you fresh moments with Him every day. All you have to do is make the time to be alone with Him.

You see, distractions and busyness will always make you dissatisfied with the moment you are in, no matter what you are doing. You will become so busy with concerns of the future that you won't be able to enjoy the moment for what it is—and that includes those special moments with the heavenly Father.

As parents, we can also let the busyness of life steal the enjoyment of special moments with our own children.

For instance, as you hold little baby Johnny in your arms, you might say, "Boy, I can't wait until little Johnny sleeps through the night!" You plug a pacifier into his mouth and exclaim wistfully, "It's going to be so great!"

Then little Johnny starts sleeping through the night. Now you say, "I can't wait until little Johnny starts to walk!"

Later on, you remark, "I can't wait until he starts to talk" and "I can't wait till he goes to kindergarten!"

Do you know what you've been doing with that kind of attitude? You have been missing all those special moments God was trying to give you with your child.

You see, your entire life is made up of moments, and every moment forms a memory. Moments can only be precious if they form a special memory. And you'll never form a special memory if you spend the whole "moment" thinking about the way you wish life could be at some point in the future.

When Jesus came to Mary and Martha's house, God was giving them a moment to be remembered for a lifetime. What a glorious memory could be formed by taking advantage of that special moment in Jesus' presence! But first, both women had a choice to make. If that visit was to be the blessing God intended for them, they both had to *choose the good portion*.

I remember very well when the Lord taught me to make that choice in my own spiritual walk. At one point in my life during a three-year period, I sensed the Lord leading me to take some extra time each day to pull aside and wait on Him. So every morning, I would go to a special place in my home to meet God. During that time, I'd just wait on the Lord and listen.

Now, it didn't seem like much was happening during those quiet times with the Lord. I didn't hear a voice from heaven or see lightning bolts streak across the sky. But those special moments with Jesus became very precious to me. And later I came to realize that just spending that time with the Lord each day brought me into a dramatic deliverance from self-dependence. I learned that each day I have to decide whether I'm going to be a Mary or a Martha—choosing "the good portion" or relying on my own efforts to work out things in my personal life.

Self-reliance is actually one of the greatest distractions and weights you can have in your life. The world teaches you that self-reliance is a virtue: "I can do this for myself. I don't need anyone." But that isn't the way of the Christian life. True Christianity is being totally dependent on Jesus. Without Him, you can do absolutely nothing. (John 15:5)

Now, it's true that a person can find a measure of success in this life by depending on his or her own efforts. But every person on the face of this earth deals with situations at one time or another that he or she cannot handle alone.

When we do try to depend on our own wisdom and strength in difficult situations, we suffer all kinds of consequences, from heart attacks to "burnout." That's why we all have to learn that Jesus is the only way. He is the great helper in times of trouble upon whom we must utterly depend. God teaches us this truth as we spend those special moments with Him.

During that period of time, God opened the way for me to get to know Him intimately and to be changed by His presence. He told me what to do; then it was up to me to choose to obey Him.

Every now and then, I think back on those times I had with the Lord in our special little meeting place. And I wonder, *What if I hadn't obeyed God by setting aside that time each morning for Him? What part of my being rooted and established in Him would have been lost?* I am just so grateful to God for giving me the strength to choose the "one thing needful" so I could grow unhindered in Him.

Living Life in "the Fast Lane"

Nothing can raise you up higher in God than hearing Jesus speak to you personally. You can learn wonderful knowledge about the Word at church, but a church service can't take the place of hearing from God yourself. It can only be a supplement to what the Lord is already saying to you in your own personal fellowship with Him.

No matter what problem you are dealing with, you can get it solved by spending time with Jesus. He can tell you exactly what to do through the Holy Spirit living on the inside of you. All you have to do is take the time to hear Him and then obey what He tells you to do.

However, too often our lifestyles are too over occupied and busy to hear the Holy Spirit when He speaks to us. We need to learn from Jesus' example as He walked this earth.

The Gospels talk about Jesus traveling from Jericho to Jerusalem, from Jerusalem to Bethany, and so on. Now, Jesus didn't have a car or even a bicycle. Everywhere He went, He *walked*. And I'm sure that as Jesus walked, He spent a lot of time communing with the Father. In fact, sometimes Jesus even went off by Himself to pray all night!

In our high-technology society, we have all sorts of time-saving items—computers, fax machines, drive-through restaurants—that are meant to give us more free time to spend in serenity and quiet. But instead, we have used these modern conveniences as a means to get more done! We have become more, *not* less, consumed with activities, interests, and our own sense of productivity. As a result, we live each day "in the fast lane," going from crisis to crisis and seldom taking the time to get rejuvenated and refreshed in God's presence.

This sad state of affairs in the Church reminds me of what Jesus said to the church of Laodicea in Revelation 3:15-19 (KJV):

> *I know thy works, that thou art neither cold nor hot: I would thou wert cold or hot. So then because thou art lukewarm, and neither cold nor hot, I will spue thee out of my mouth.*
>
> *Because thou sayest, I am rich, and increased with goods, and have need of nothing; and knowest not that thou art wretched, and miserable, and poor, and blind, and naked: I counsel thee to buy of me gold tried in the fire, that thou mayest be rich; and white raiment, that thou mayest be clothed, and that the shame of thy nakedness do not appear; and anoint thine eyes with eyesalve, that thou mayest see.*
>
> *As many as I love, I rebuke and chasten: be zealous therefore, and repent.*

I believe this passage is prophetic for this hour we're living in. Busyness is one of the greatest things the Church of the Lord Jesus Christ has to overcome. Our overpacked schedules continually distract us from spending time with God, requiring us to "keep the pedal to the metal" all the time and keeping us lukewarm in our spiritual walk.

The Lord started dealing with me years ago about simplifying my life. He asked me this question: *If I asked you to pick up and move to Israel tomorrow, would you be able to do it?*

"Are you kidding, Lord?" I said. "I have too much stuff! I mean, I'd need several months just to pack and set up a caravan of four airplanes to transport it all!"

That experience taught me something about myself. My life was too complicated to be free to obey God, no matter what He asked me to do.

I'm not the exception to the rule either. The same is true for most of us who live in today's society. We allow our lives to get so complicated that we are hindered from obeying God.

God speaks to our hearts and says, "I want you to take a quiet moment to reflect on some things I've been teaching you." Or He says, "I want you to set aside some time to lay this matter on the altar and let Me talk to you about it."

But we tell the Lord, "I don't have time, God. I'm too busy!" Then in the next breath, we pray, "Oh, God, help me!"

And God answers, "I'm trying to help you, child. That's why I've been calling you to come aside and spend time with Me!"

Simplify Your Life

Soon after I was born again, my husband, Mac, helped me work my way out of unnecessary busyness and distractions. He said to me, "Lynne, write down on a sheet of paper everything you're doing right now in one column; then write everything you *want* to do in another column."

After I did what Mac had asked, he said, "Now look at those two lists and see if they line up."

Do you know what I found out? I wasn't doing one thing I wanted to do!

That may sound amazing to you, but the same thing is true in most people's lives. That's why so many Christians don't experience any joy or peace. They are dissatisfied and frustrated with all the unnecessary clutter in their lives!

Years after making that list, I was still learning this same hard lesson. I was walking in the woods one day, and the Lord opened up Psalm 119:130 (KJV) to me: "The entrance of thy words giveth light." I was so thrilled by that one truth! But then I read the rest of the verse: "It giveth understanding unto the simple." I realized that God's words give light and understanding to the *simple*, not to the *complicated*. So as I walked through the woods, I started thinking, *What can I do to simplify my life so I can spend more time with God?*

I had been walking in the shadow of trees for a while when suddenly I walked out on an open field where the sunlight shone down on me unhindered. I thought, *That's just the way it is in our lives as Christians.*

The shadows of those trees represent our crowded, busy schedules that keep the light of God from shining through into our hearts!

Just think about those mornings when you know you have a very busy day ahead of you. As soon as you sit down to read the Word and pray, the demands of your day suddenly start pressing into your thoughts. Soon you become so dissatisfied and agitated that your brain isn't able to concentrate on what you're reading.

What has happened? The enemy of your soul has used busyness and distractions to steal from you a special moment that God wanted to give you. You could have left that time with the Lord knowing Him a little better and walking in an increase of His power and presence in your life. But instead, you get up to go about your day feeling frustrated and "out of whack."

Once stolen, those moments of time God wants to give you can never be recaptured. You can't videotape or record on an audiocassette the fullness of God's manifested power and presence. However, you can choose to never let the enemy steal those moments from you again!

Your Determined Purpose: to Know Him

Perhaps you can see now why it's so important that you regulate your life to include a lot of time with Jesus. The truth is, there are more distractions coming against the Church in this age than ever before. You have to *choose* to make fellowship with God your highest priority. You do that by following the apostle Paul's example.

Paul understood well how much he needed the reality of God's presence in his life in order to fulfill the task set before him. That's why he had a divine safeguard in his life to keep him out of trouble. That divine safeguard is found in Philippians 3:10:

> *[For my determined purpose is] that I may know Him [that I may progressively become more deeply and intimately acquainted with Him, perceiving and recognizing and understanding the wonders of His Person more strongly and more clearly], And that I may in that same way come to know the power outflowing from His resurrection.*

Notice the progression of increase in Paul's relationship with Jesus. He never reached a place in his spiritual walk where he became satisfied with his growth. Also, notice that Paul *didn't* say, "My determined purpose in life is that I may know the Scriptures" or "that I may know what Brother So-and-so said." Paul wanted to experience God's presence *for himself.*

Paul's determined purpose wasn't to preach the Gospel, to win the lost, or to heal the sick, although those are all high and lofty goals. His determined purpose in life was *to know Jesus.*

And do you know when Paul actually wrote those words? Three weeks before he died! He didn't just say that at the beginning of his Christian walk when the zeal of God was consuming him. Even at the end of his course, in his final days on this earth, Paul was still saying, "The entire purpose of my life has gone in one direction, and that is to know God."

If your determined purpose is to obtain material wealth, build a ministry, do well in your business, or give huge amounts of money for the Gospel, you have already missed the mark. You cannot increase in your spiritual walk as long as your purpose in life is misplaced.

All those things are good in themselves. But Jesus doesn't want a ministry. He doesn't want a business. He doesn't want money. He wants *you*. He died for you in order to have fellowship with you. When Jesus has you—in other words, when knowing Him is truly your determined purpose in life—He has everything else in your life as well!

The Lord once spoke to my heart and said, "I'm not interested in your building a ministry. I'm interested in your becoming a person just like Me."

When the Holy Spirit said that to me, I really started examining my priorities and motives as a Christian. *Just exactly what am I living for?* I thought.

You see, there are few things that are "enough" in life. It's wonderful to receive the material needs or the finances you're believing God for, but there is always something else to believe for. There never seems to be "enough."

But there is one thing that is enough. Matthew 10:25 (KJV) tells us what it is: "It is enough for the disciple that he be as his master." It is enough to be like Jesus.

But to become like Jesus, we must *experience* Him. We can't just go through life with our heads filled with knowledge *about* Him. If we don't put the Word to work in our lives, our Christianity has just become another system of philosophy.

And understand this: You get to know Jesus by degrees. The more you know Him, the more you become like Him. And the more you become like Him, the more you are able to give out His life and His love to others.

Your Life Is a Result of Choices

It's your choice whether or not you're going to know all God wants you to know or have all He wants you to have in life. God has a big "promised land" of blessings just waiting for you to possess. He has a good plan for your life that He wants you to fulfill. But in order to possess your spiritual inheritance, you will have to make a quality decision every single day of your life to fellowship with God.

Of course, you don't have to make that decision. You can choose anything you want to choose. But it's important to realize that your life will be a result of whatever choices you make. Whether or not you walk in God's highest and best for your life ultimately depends on how you answer this question for yourself: *Am I going to let distractions keep me from spending time alone with God?*

How much time do you need each day to fellowship with God? All I can tell you is that you need *time enough*. What is time enough for you? I don't know. I only know what is time enough for me. However, I'd venture to say that if you would tithe your time to God, you would rise to a higher place in God than you could have ever imagined!

You can make the decision right now to set aside time to sit at Jesus' feet. You can "choose the good portion," just as Mary did. But remember—tomorrow you will have to make that same choice all over again. That's how you progressively become more deeply and intimately acquainted with God!

Chapter 5

Stay Hungry for God

When Moses stood before the burning bush, he asked the Lord a question based on his own sense of inadequacy: "Who am I, that I should go to Pharaoh and bring the Israelites out of Egypt?" (Exodus 3:11). The Lord's answer to Moses is very significant:

> *I will surely be with you; and this shall be the sign to you that I have sent you: when you have brought the people out of Egypt, you shall serve God on this mountain* [Horeb, or Sinai].
>
> EXODUS 3:12

God promised Moses that He would surely be with him every step of the way. His presence would be the sign Moses needed that he was sent by God to deliver Israel from Egypt.

You see, God's presence upon your life is what marks you. His presence marked Moses' life, and it certainly marked Jesus' life. Jesus' ministry was approved and confirmed by the presence of God that continually accompanied Him. As for the early church, Mark 16:20 (KJV) says, "And they went forth, and preached every where, the Lord working with them, and confirming the word with signs following." That means the presence of the Lord marked the early disciples' ministry wherever they went.

How Hungry Are You?

The same is true for today. God's presence is what marks us in a lost and dying world. And His manifest presence is readily available in this hour. All we have to do is open our hearts, and the presence of God will come in and change us from glory to glory.

However, there is one requirement to walking in the presence of God as a way of life. You have to stay desperately hungry for God—not hungry for spectacular manifestations, but hungry for *Him*.

If you are spiritually hungry, you are full of spiritual vitality. You are thirsting and hungering after God all the time. The Holy Spirit is moving on your behalf in every realm of life.

That's how I was when I first got saved. I wanted to read a chapter of the Bible every single day. But as I became more acquainted with the Lord, one chapter wasn't enough for me anymore; I needed *three* chapters. Then three chapters weren't enough for me. I needed more and more, not less and less of God's Word.

If you're hungry for God, you need more and more of His presence working in your life. But how do you make sure you *stay* hungry for Him? The most important thing I can tell you is this: It's important that you regularly take spiritual inventory of yourself.

Check daily to see how hungry you are for God. Look at what you focus most of your time, thoughts, and energy on. Ask yourself these questions:

- *What is my purpose in life today?*
- *Am I doing what I'm supposed to be doing about my fellowship with God?*
- *Am I increasing in God?*
- *Am I reaching out on the inside, crying out for more of Him?*
- *Do I have more faith today than I did yesterday?*

When you are checking yourself daily with honest questions like these, you will quickly catch yourself if you start veering from your divine purpose. That's what Ephesians 5:15 (AMP) means when it says, "Look carefully then how you walk! Live purposefully and worthily and accurately, not as the unwise and witless, but as wise (sensible, intelligent people)."

Sometimes you have to shake yourself awake! Don't just plod along on the treadmill of life, never checking up to see how you are doing in God's eyes.

Take spiritual inventory and then reorder your life so you can become rooted in Him.

Few Christians bother to take spiritual inventory of themselves on a regular basis. As a result, backsliding is rampant in the Church today. Fortunately, there is something that can cure the most hardened backslider, and that is *the presence of God.*

If a person will stay in God's presence long enough and frequently enough to stay saturated, he won't yield to the influences of the world. God's presence will continually change him from glory to glory—*as long as he stays hungry.*

Think about how you view a lack of appetite in the natural. For instance, if your baby stops eating, your first thought is that he or she may be sick. A loss of appetite is often the first sign that something is abnormal. Healthy people are hungry people.

Well, it's exactly the same way in the spiritual realm. If you go for periods of time without being hungry for God, for His Word, or for His glory to be manifested in your life—*that* is a bad indicator. You can be sure that something is wrong in your walk with the Lord.

A great evangelist once said something about himself along these same lines. He prayed with more people in his lifetime than we could ever imagine. Yet he still said that he *must* have the manifest presence of God. If he sensed that presence beginning to leave, or if he could not feel the presence of God, he knew something was wrong and would start fasting and praying. He would call the people who pray for him and tell them to pray three or four times a day—in the morning, at noon, and at night—until he could sense that manifested presence again.

I know how he felt because I have never been hungrier for more of God's presence in my life than I am right now. I'm hungry for 2 Corinthians 3:18 to be fulfilled in *me*. I'm hungry to be changed by His presence from glory to glory.

Don't "Run on Fumes"

Why is it that we sometimes stagnate in our walk with the Lord? I have found that when the Spirit of God is moving in our lives, the things of the Spirit become very familiar to us. And if we're not careful, we can let them become so commonplace that we stop expecting. We stop using our faith to change. And when we stop using our faith, when we stop expecting, when we stop being hungry—that's when we stagnate spiritually.

Let me tell you what happens to a lot of Christians. They get born again, Spirit-filled, and delivered from bondage. They're on fire, going one hundred percent for God! They wouldn't miss church for anything. God is mightily blessing them. Their lives have begun to change because of the Word. They're telling everyone, "I'm so glad I'm a Christian!"

Then all of a sudden, they start getting comfortable. With that comfort comes a little bit of laziness. Then they develop the attitude, *Well, if I miss a day of reading my Bible, it doesn't really make that much difference. And I prayed yesterday, so I don't have to pray today. God will understand. He knows how busy I am!*

A little later they say, "I don't believe I'll go to church tonight. I'll get the tape to find out what went on in the service."

Gradually these Christians have gone from excited to comfortable to lazy to lukewarm. Now they start growing cold to the things of God. Where is the fire that burned in their hearts? Where is the passion and the love they once had for Jesus?

Meanwhile, their lives become more and more complicated with busyness and the pursuit of worldly things. In the end, they become backslidden and don't even realize how it happened. They are emotionally and physically drained. They have ceased to increase in God.

My husband, Mac, often chastises me for running my car on empty. He's constantly telling me, "Lynne, I never get in your car when it has more than a fourth of a tank of gas. And most of the time, it has a lot less than that! You're usually running on fumes!"

Too many Christians run on fumes spiritually. They hurry through their days with very little Word, no prayer, and no manifested presence of God. They live on the ragged edge of life, squeezing through situations in their own strength instead of pushing through them with the power of God. They still have the title of Christian, but they are living far below that standard.

Don't ever get satisfied with where you are in your walk with God. Don't ever start thinking, *I'm filled, and I don't need any more.* Stay hungry every minute of every day for more of Him.

That's the way God expects us to live in this hour. He has given us a standard to live by—to constantly increase in God. We are not to stray off that standard even an inch!

In order to live by that divine standard, I've learned over the years to always treat myself like a dry sponge. I may even be filled with God's presence at the moment, but I still think of myself as a dry sponge that's desperately in need of more Holy Ghost rain. Why do I do that? Because if I start thinking of myself as already filled, I won't go any further in the process of becoming filled with all the fullness of God.

Back for Another Dose of God

Moses was a "dry sponge" too. Remember, he climbed up Mount Sinai and spent forty days and forty nights there in the manifested presence of God. When he finally came off that mountain, he had a ten-point message on tablets of stone that he was going to give to his congregation of about three million people.

But as Moses walked down off that mountain, he heard dancing and music. Then he saw the people worshiping a golden calf, and he lost his sanctification! Although he had come fresh from the glory and the presence of God, Moses had a little temper fit in which he broke the tablets of stone. (Exodus 32:19)

Then in Exodus 33:12-13, he entreated God, "Lord, I found favor in Your sight, but there's just one thing I don't know. Are You going with me to take these stiff-necked people to the Promised Land? Lord, I have to know You more progressively, to become more intimately acquainted with the wonders of Your person."

After forty days and forty nights, Moses was still not satisfied. He was still seeking that everlasting, ever-living presence of almighty God!

Then in Exodus 33:18, he cried out to the Lord again, saying, "Lord, show me Your glory!"

In other words, Moses was saying, "I know I just spent forty days with You, Lord. But when I came back down here to this mess, I had a temper fit and broke the tablets of stone. Now what am I going to do?"

Do you know what God said to Moses? "Come up again." (Exodus 34:2) Moses needed another dose of God's presence!

Often Christians think, *I'm going to yield to God. I'll get over in His presence once or twice, and that will be enough to change what needs to be changed in me.* But it doesn't work that way.

The first forty days Moses was up on Mount Sinai, he received some temporary help. But then he went back up on the mountain for forty more days—a total of eighty days. That's almost three months of being in the manifest presence of God! And when Moses came down off the mountain the second time, he even had to use a veil to hide the brilliance of God's glory on his face! (Exodus 34:29,33) Moses had returned to his people a changed man.

Why is that? Because the glory of God will change you if you will just *stay in His presence*.

This was one of many encounters Moses had with God during the years he led Israel—miraculous, marvelous encounters. But Moses never stayed stagnant. He didn't stop and park at some point in his walk with God. He kept moving on until he finished his course.

Of course, Moses was a great man of God. But Moses' holy hunger should be even more evident in us, God's chosen, blood-bought, redeemed, new covenant people. Jesus paid the price with His own blood for us so we would continually hunger after Him.

A Family Transformed by God's Presence

I heard a testimony that thrilled my heart concerning the power of staying in God's presence. A woman got up in church one morning to give a testimony about God's work in her family. Sixteen family members also stood up with her as she told their story.

This woman and her sixteen family members all lived close to each other. Even though they were all Christians, these relatives had always been embroiled in terrible strife and division, fighting continually among themselves.

Then this woman started attending revival services at a particular church. Soon her daughter started coming with her. Then slowly over the next eighteen months, all sixteen family members began to attend the services.

"We continually came to church so we could be saturated with God's presence," the woman said. "We knew it was going to take more than one dose to change us!"

The woman continued, "Yesterday, for the first time in our lives, we all spent Christmas together in a spirit of love. I want to give glory to the presence of God!"

"Stay in the Anointing"

I'll tell you another good reason to saturate yourself in the presence of God: It's the place you want to be when you need a healing in your body.

A precious brother in the Lord whom Mac and I know had some kind of neurological problem that affected his nervous system and caused all kinds of muscle problems in his body. He told us that three separate times the Lord spoke to his spirit, saying, *I'm going to tell you how to get healed: Stay in the anointing.*

That's good counsel. I heard about a woman who followed that same divine counsel and received her healing at the revival in Pensacola, Florida.

Years ago when this woman's child was about two years old, he ran out in front of a moving car. The mother jumped in front of her son and pushed him out of the way. But in doing so she fell, and the car ran over one side of her face.

In the years that followed, the woman had to undergo many painful surgeries and treatments in an attempt to repair her face. But despite it all, she remained in constant, terrible pain. She had stood in numerous healing lines, and several ministers had laid hands on her.

This woman also knew the Word of God well, including all the healing scriptures.

Then one day she heard about the Pensacola revival and decided to start attending the services. She made herself available to the presence of God at that revival every single night.

This woman was *hungry,* and she was *available.* Those are two big words to take hold of, because a person won't ever be very hungry if he never avails himself to God.

So the woman went to the revival services every single night for months, saturating herself in the presence of God. And by the time I heard her give her testimony, she was completely, one-hundred-percent healed!

Another man who was totally blind came to my sister's church for three months every single night during a revival. The lady who was ministering during the revival laid hands on him many times during that three months. Every night the blind man sat in God's presence. Every night he'd say, "I will see." And at the end of the three months, he was totally healed!

You see, there is a saturation level of God's presence that you often have to attain before you or your circumstances can be changed. The Bible says the way we will be changed into Jesus' image from glory to glory is by the manifested presence of God. And since that's what the Bible says, it would behoove us to get in God's presence as much and as often as we can!

Taking Spiritual Inventory

That's why it's so important to take spiritual inventory of our lives on a regular basis. We need to ask ourselves questions that will help us locate ourselves spiritually, such as these: "Do I really know Jesus? Do I really want to know Him? Is He Lord of every area of my life? What am I worshiping? Am I worshiping myself? My children? My job? What is my purpose in life? Is my determined purpose to know Jesus, as it was Paul's determined purpose? Or do I have another purpose that I pursue with greater desire?"

If you start asking yourself pointed questions like these, I guarantee you'll get really hungry for God really fast! There is so much more God wants to give you, but in order to receive it, you have to become desperately hungry for more of Him. God isn't going to come and interrupt your life without your permission. He isn't going to intervene unless you ask Him to.

So take the time to get quiet in your heart and tell Him, "Intervene, Lord. Change me, Jesus. More than anything else in the whole world, I desire to finish my course and fulfill my call. So I'm asking You, Lord, to make me hungry for more of You."

Chapter 6

Cultivating Holy Hunger

I've come to a place in my life where I realize that I am totally inadequate in myself to do what God has called me to do. I thought I'd never get to that place, but I'm finally there.

You see, when you start dying to yourself, your self rebels. There's no doubt about it—it's hard to die to your own self-will. Nevertheless, you have to do it. Paul himself said, "I die daily" (1 Corinthians 15:31). In other words, Paul was saying, "To walk in the realm of the spirit, I have to crucify my flesh at every turn."

The same is true for you. You will have to crucify your flesh every single day. Why? Because your flesh will try to pull against the Holy Spirit living inside you every chance it gets!

For instance, you wake up one morning and decide, "Bless God, I'm going to fast and pray all day today!" As soon as those words are out of your mouth, something happens to tempt you to give up on that decision. Maybe the doorbell rings. You open the door and find your neighbor standing there with a plate of chocolate chip cookies. What do you have to do at that moment? *Crucify your flesh.*

Or one Sunday morning, you look out the window and discover it's cold, dark, and snowing outside. What does your flesh want to do? It wants to pull the covers over your head and stay right there in bed! It certainly doesn't want to go to church!

But the only way you can ever walk in the Spirit and increase in the things of God is to first crucify those fleshly inclinations. Therefore, you have to stay hungry for more of God. As long as you are hungry, it will be much easier to allow that dying process to take place in your life. And then God will start to create a whole new you in the image of Jesus!

We can see how God goes about creating in Genesis 1:1-3 KJV:

> *In the beginning God created the heaven and the earth. And the earth was without form, and void; and darkness was upon the face of the deep. And the Spirit of God moved upon the face of the waters. And God said, Let there be light: and there was light.*

The same principle of creation applies to God's work in you. When you become void of your own self-will and you realize that nothing is left except Jesus to accomplish His will in you, then the Spirit of God can start moving on you. He starts to create what *He* wants to create on the inside of you. That's when deep change can begin.

Deep Calls Unto Deep

To reach that place where self-will has died and God is given free rein to create His will in you, you have to cultivate a deep, abiding hunger for His presence in your life. The psalmist in Psalm 42:1-2 possessed that kind of hunger:

As the hart pants and longs for the water brooks, so I pant and long for You, O God. My inner self thirsts for God, for the living God. When shall I come and behold the face of God?

The words of this psalmist show us the depth of spiritual hunger that should drive each of us into the presence of God. Our hearts should thirst and hunger for God the same way a deer pants for water on a hot, dry day.

Verse 7 goes on to say this:

[Roaring] deep calls to [roaring] deep at the thunder of Your waterspouts; all Your breakers and Your rolling waves have gone over me.

When a person is truly hungry, something deep down inside of him begins to call on God for something more. He might not even know what he is calling out for. But God knows.

Take healing, for instance. The reason you call out for healing from deep within your heart is that your spirit knows a healing is there to call forth. You wouldn't be yearning or thirsting after healing in your heart if there were no healing available to be obtained.

The same is true when your heart cries out for more of God. The "deep" in you is calling out to know the depths of God because there is always more to be known of Him. And nothing but more of God's presence in your life will satisfy that deep hunger inside.

My Own Journey to Find More of God

More than twenty years ago, before I'd ever heard of the baptism in the Holy Spirit, my soul longed after God. I had never heard of speaking in tongues. I had never heard of demonstrations of God's power. Nevertheless, my heart cried out for more of God. My spirit wept to know Him better.

I didn't know I was cultivating a holy hunger. I didn't even know what I was asking for. I just wanted to know Jesus more and more and more.

The only thing I knew in my heart to do was pray. I would pray for people as far as I could with my understanding. But I always sensed something was missing when I finished praying, although I didn't have words for it. It was such a frustration to me. I wanted more expression in my communication with the Father, but all I could say was "Lord, help me!"

I was so hungry for whatever I was missing. I found out later the missing element was the baptism in the Holy Spirit, but at the time, I didn't know that. I didn't even know how to ask God for the baptism in the Holy Spirit. I just cried out to God day and night, asking Him to show me more of Him.

Then late one night, I couldn't stay in bed because my longing for God had gotten so big in me. I was so hungry and thirsty inside that I didn't know what to do. I thought it would help if I got up and went to our little den to pray.

I hurried into the den, fell into an easy chair, and began to sob, "Help me, God. I'm so hungry for You. I just want to know You, God. Please teach me how to pray."

That's all I said to Him. But the deep in me was calling out for something I didn't understand with my mind. I knew God was bigger than what I had ever seen or experienced. I wanted that bigger part of God with all my heart.

As I sat in that chair weeping, it felt as if my spirit were being wrung out like a towel. I kept sobbing, "God, help me. I just want to know You." Suddenly the power of God came into that room like lightning and started shaking me. It shook me and shook me until it had shaken me down to the floor. Then waves of glory began to hit me again and again!

Now, I didn't know anything about waves of glory. I didn't know about the lightnings of God. But these manifestations of God's presence came because I was a hungry soul. The deep in me was calling out for the greater depths of God.

Then the fire of God began to burn in me. It felt like I was burning up! I even looked at my skin to see if it was on fire!

All of a sudden, a beautiful language began to flow out of me like a river. I'm not talking about five syllables of baby talk. A great river of God flowed out of me in a full-blown language I didn't know.

I stayed in the glory of that experience for a long time. Later I asked God, "Lord, why did You manifest Yourself so dramatically to me that night?"

"Because you were calling out for it," the Lord told me. "You get whatever you're hungry for."

You Get What You're Hungry For

That's true for all of us. In other words, whatever is number one—whatever is the biggest thing on the inside of us—will eventually overtake us until we think of nothing else. And because of the power that is resident within us, we will receive whatever our soul hungers after. If we're hungry for worldly things, that's what we're going to get. If we hunger after a new car, eventually we will get a new car.

That's why there's something better than worldly possessions. There's something better than a new car.

There is Jesus who made all the parts of the car! He's the one who knows everything about everything. And when you get Jesus, you have everything.

I'm telling you, the deep in you should be continually calling out for the depths of God. Don't just go to church to hear some preacher regurgitate a Bible truth that will apply a little salve to your conscience. Go to church because you're hungry for God—hungry to hear His voice, hungry for Him to move on your behalf.

If you're hungry for a miracle, you'll receive a miracle. If you're hungry to know God, you'll find Him and you'll come to know Him. He will make Himself real to you. You'll get what you are hungry for.

Oh, how the Church of the Lord Jesus Christ needs God to make Himself real! How the Church needs to cultivate holy hunger!

Don't Live on Past Experiences

One day I was reading the Song of Solomon, and I told God, "I want to be just like that woman in the third chapter of Song of Solomon."

This woman said, "I'm leaving all the ease and luxury of my home, and I'm going out to find him whom my soul loves." (Song of Solomon 3:1,2) She had just been with her beloved that afternoon, but that wasn't enough for her. Her longing to be with him drove her out to look for him again.

People get in trouble in their spiritual walk because they don't have that kind of lover's heart for Jesus. They experience God's presence in a special way one day, and then they think, *That experience should hold me for a while.* Then instead of constantly seeking after more of Jesus, they keep referring back to that one experience as their defining moment: "I remember when God did something special in my life. Let me tell you about it."

No, don't let yourself live on past experiences with your Father. Live your life centered around Him every day. Be grateful for what God did for you yesterday. Be grateful for what He did for you this afternoon. But don't be satisfied with that. Keep your hand stretched out for more of Him.

Also, don't ever be content to settle for just the tinsel of God's kingdom. Now, I believe in prosperity. In fact, I'm a prosperous person. But I don't seek after prosperity. I seek after Jesus, the one who is everything. And in my seeking, *He* makes me prosperous.

I also don't seek for answers in my life. I seek Jesus because He is the answer to every question. If I seek Him, I have all the answers.

I seek after eternal life, the life that's in God. The world tells us all kinds of things about life. It tells us life is gusto, and success and prosperity. But I'm telling you, my friend, *life is Jesus.* When you find Him, you find life.

Get to Know the God of the Book

Some people think that once they are filled with the Holy Spirit, that's it. That's the epitome of experiencing God.

But the truth is, it's just the beginning. We've only begun to explore the depths of God when we receive the baptism in the Holy Ghost.

I know from personal experience that this is true. After I was baptized in the Holy Spirit, I was hungrier for God than ever. So I kept on seeking to know Him better. I prayed, "Oh, God, You've got to reveal Yourself to me more fully. I want to know You!"

And in His wonderful, sweet way, the Lord spoke to me in my spirit, saying, *I am the God of the Book. I'll speak to you out of the Book.*

So what did I do? Well, I *didn't* walk by the Book on my nightstand every now and then so I could pat it and say, "God, You're the God of the Book. Good for You!"

No, I got into the Book, and I started reading it. I began to devour my Bible, expecting all the while to find God in it. And sure enough, I found Him there! I found out who He is. I saw that He is the God who created the heavens and the earth. He's the God who split the Red Sea. He's the God who rained manna down from heaven for His children. He's the God who healed the blind, the crippled, and the maimed. He's the power behind Paul's handkerchiefs and aprons, Stephen's signs and wonders, and Peter and John's miracles.

I kept reading and reading and reading the Book until I could finally say, "This God I read about is the God I know personally."

And now that the God of the Book is living on the inside of me, I cannot be satisfied until I see the things I've read in the Book manifested in my life and in the Church. I will not stop until hell is shaken!

Too many times I see the people of God sitting back in complacency. They've gotten lazy. They're not reading about or praying to the God of the Book. Therefore, they're not hungry to have His presence manifested in their lives.

But God wants to be the God of the Book to every one of His children. He wants to be *your* Healer. He wants to be *your* Miracle Worker. He wants *you* to walk in the glory He has called you to walk in.

For you to experience God in these ways, however, you have to cultivate an insatiable hunger to know Him for yourself. You have to spend much time in His presence. You have to find and develop the place of intimate fellowship with Him, for that is the place where He speaks to your heart and changes you from the inside out.

Hungering After Holiness

I want to walk in the fullness of God's glory on this earth. I want Him to manifest His power in my life every time I come to church! I want to be a spiritual vacuum, void of everything but Jesus so His presence can fill my life.

When you become a vacuum, the wind of the Holy Spirit can start blowing on you and changing you into the image of Jesus. He can do all kinds of marvelous, miraculous things for you.

Personally, I'm looking for a big wind and a huge Holy Ghost rainstorm to blow through my life! I want to see signs and wonders and miracles manifested in our church and in the body of Christ because that's the kind of God I serve. He's the God of the Book, a miracle-working God!

But if we're going to see God's presence manifested in our midst to that extent, we have to cultivate a holy, desperate hunger for God. We have to get so hungry that we inspire others to hunger after Him.

I remember a story about Dr. Lilian B. Yeomans, a doctor who later became a great evangelist. Dr. Yeomans didn't care whether or not people called her a great evangelist. Her soul cried and her heart hungered for the holiness of God. She desired to be holy more than anything else, so she always prayed in that direction. She hungered and thirsted after holiness.

One day she and some other believers attended a meeting in someone's home.

At the meeting, Dr. Yeomans started talking about holiness, the sanctified life, and the grace and power of God. A man who was at the meeting later related, "Before I heard Dr. Yeomans speak, I loved and respected God. But I was self-satisfied. I was happy and successful, possessing all the things that accompany material success.

"Then Dr. Yeomans began to talk to all of us in that room about the holy life. And it wasn't her words or her logic of argument that struck my heart so strongly. It was what I saw in her. There was something in her that made me hungry for more of God. I saw the living Spirit of God. I saw the Spirit of holiness on her."

The man continued, "I got so hungry that I fell to my knees and began to pray. From that day to this, all the people who were present at the meeting remember me for that prayer I prayed. Years later, one of the people came to me and said, 'I remember the prayer you prayed as you listened to that woman and then fell on your face before God.'"

This man said he prayed until the rafters shook and the fire struck, until the power came down and all their lives were sanctified by the power and grace of God in that instant.

That is what spiritual hunger will do for every believer. Oh, how we need to be hungry!

Blessed Are They Who Hunger

In Matthew 5:3 (KJV), Jesus said, "Blessed are the poor in spirit: for theirs is the kingdom of heaven." I used to ask God, "Lord, who are the poor in spirit? Is that verse talking about those who don't have any money?"

I finally came to understand what that verse meant. Just think about what poor people have to do. Of necessity, their entire quest in life is to find basic provisions to survive. All their energies and attention have to go toward finding ways to provide food for their family's table.

In the same way, when we are poor in spirit, we are constantly looking for more of Jesus to feed our spirits. The Bible says we are greatly blessed as we cultivate that continual state of spiritual hunger: "Blessed are they which do hunger and thirst after righteousness: for they shall be filled" (Matthew 5:6 KJV).

My soul longs after God. I'm looking for Him. I'm looking for His appearance. I'm looking for signs and wonders. I'm looking for the manifestations of spiritual gifts to hasten the day of the Lord. I'm watching. I'm waiting. Are you?

If you are not yet a diligent seeker of God, I recommend that you get on your face before God and pray, "God, make me hungry." Get into the Word and find the God of the Book. Shut yourself away with Him in a secret place where He can start talking to you once again about who He is. He has things to say to you that you will hear no other way.

Chapter 7

Walking With God

Did you know that Enoch and Noah of the Old Testament knew a secret most Christians today haven't figured out yet? These two men discovered *how to walk with God*. That doesn't mean they visited His presence once a week or every so often when it was convenient. The Bible says they walked with Him continually, day in and day out, as a way of life.

Let's look at what the Bible says about these two men of God:

> When Enoch was 65 years old, Methuselah was born. Enoch walked [in habitual fellowship]

with God after the birth of Methuselah 300 years and had other sons and daughters.

GENESIS 5:21,22

> But Noah found grace (favor) in the eyes of the Lord. This is the history of the generations of Noah. Noah was a just and righteous man, blameless in his [evil] generation; Noah walked [in habitual fellowship] with God.

GENESIS 6:8,9

If Enoch and Noah knew how to walk with God in habitual fellowship, how much more should the Church of the Lord Jesus Christ know how to do the same?

You see, the greatest work of Calvary was the access into God's presence that Jesus' death on the cross provided for us. That right of access wasn't just for brief, momentary visits so we could get a spiritual "fix" and then return to a natural life of deprivation. No, Jesus died so we could *walk* in the fire and the glory of God's presence every moment of every day.

The Call for a Deeper Walk With God

That's why the Holy Spirit is calling us out of a superficial Christianity into a deeper walk of intimate fellowship with Him. I'm talking about the kind of walk in which we examine our lives every single day. We learn to talk to God honestly. We don't pretend that our faults are someone else's problem. We allow the Holy Spirit to turn the light of His presence and His Word on every area of our lives, and we obey Him when He tells us to change.

Paul talks about walking with God on this level in Galatians 5:24-25:

> *And those who belong to Christ Jesus (the Messiah) have crucified the flesh (the godless human nature) with its passions and appetites and desires. If we live by the [Holy] Spirit, let us also walk by the Spirit. [If by the Holy Spirit we have our life in God, let us go forward walking in line, our conduct controlled by the Spirit.]*

I often see people who avoid talking to God all the time during our church prayer meetings. As soon as I say, "Let's pray," these people always start praying in tongues. Why do they do that? Often the reason is that they don't know how to talk to God out of their hearts. They don't know how to talk to Him as their best friend.

Now, I'm not coming against tongues in any way. I pray in tongues all the time. But when it's time to fellowship with the Father, we shouldn't put our mouths on "automatic pilot" and start praying in tongues while we allow our minds to make our grocery lists, plan tomorrow's schedule, and so forth. We need to learn how to talk to God as our loving Father—to bare our hearts before Him and lay everything out on the altar.

Where is that level of intimacy in the Church today? My heart is crying out to see people enter into that kind of fellowship with the Father, to know the joy and delight of just being in His presence.

But you don't reach that place by living a frivolous lifestyle. You get there by walking closely with God.

So let's talk about what it means to walk with God on a continual basis. Enoch and Noah may have known sweet fellowship with God, but we can experience a far greater level of intimacy with Him. After all, He is our Father, and we are His blood-bought, redeemed children.

That's why I always say to the Lord, "Enoch isn't going to have anything on me, Lord!" You can make that same determination as you learn how to walk intimately with God.

Learning to Walk With God

My introduction into learning to walk with God took place that night the glory of the Lord filled our den and filled me with the Holy Spirit. I didn't know what had happened to me; I just knew it was something of God. I didn't have words to describe it to anyone, and I didn't know who to ask what had happened to me.

Then I thought of a lady named Michelle who worked in my husband's office. (Of course, Mac and I weren't in the ministry at the time.) This woman said, "Praise the Lord!" all the time, so I thought she'd be the most likely candidate to ask.

I called this woman on the telephone and said, "Michelle, something has happened to me." However,

I didn't know how to tell her *what* had happened, so I just started praying in tongues.

I had no idea Michelle was Pentecostal, but suddenly I heard her phone drop to the floor. Then I heard her shoes tapping on the hardwood floor as she ran through her house shouting. She shouted and praised the Lord all over her house while I listened on my end of the telephone. I found out later that Michelle had been praying for my husband and me to receive more of God through the baptism of the Holy Ghost.

Anyway, with my baptism in the Holy Ghost came a greater sense of God's call on my life and an even greater desire to pray. As a result, the Holy Spirit became more active in my life. The Lord would bring people to my heart to pray for, and I began to yield more and more to prayer.

But I was still very new to the things of God. I didn't know anything about the Word or what was happening to me. Therefore, I wasn't as obedient to pray as I should have been. I was just this young, ignorant woman trying to get to know God's ways on her own.

A Supernatural Lesson in Prayer

Then something happened that taught me a hard but valuable lesson about walking with God in the area of prayer. Mac and I had some friends who were missionaries to Albania. At the time (and to a large extent still today), Albania was very bound up spiritually. If a person got caught preaching the Gospel there, he was in very big trouble. But despite the danger, our missionary friends felt called to go minister to the Albanian people.

Before our friends left, they called and asked me to pray for them while they were gone. I said yes, but then I forgot about my promise and wasn't really obedient to pray for them. I'd just lift them up to the Lord in a casual way once in a while.

Then one night I couldn't sleep because these missionaries' faces kept coming before me. I tossed and turned all night long but never really yielded to prayer. I just thought about them a lot through the long hours of the night.

But God never puts someone on your heart just so you can think warmly about them. Having warm feelings about people doesn't do them any good.

The next morning as I was getting our children off to school, I received a telephone call from the missionaries' secretary. She cried as she told us that our friends had been taken into custody by the authorities. The husband had been beaten and thrown into prison, and the secretary didn't know exactly where the wife was.

When I heard that bad report, the conviction of God came on me more strongly than ever before. I literally could not say a word. I was almost in shock because I knew in my heart that somehow if I had prayed, I could have stopped this tragedy from coming to pass. I don't know how I knew it, but I knew it.

I went into the bedroom and closed the door behind me very carefully and quietly. Then I fell on my bed and began to cry as if my heart would break.

You know, Jesus is so wonderful. He saw me in my distress over this situation, and He came to me in a great visitation of which I shall never forget. In that visitation, He shared with me the priority prayer held in His own heart. He taught me about Holy Ghost prayer and praying without ceasing. Finally, He talked to me about a place in the Spirit where I could walk continually with God. Until that moment, I didn't even know what it meant to walk with God!

During that supernatural experience, Jesus consoled and comforted me by His presence. But even afterward, the glory of God remained in my spirit, compelling me to pray.

This was the period of time when I began to set aside time just to spend with the Lord. I didn't know what to do or how to do it. I just knew I had to pray.

Not too many tapes or books were available at the time that could have taught me about Holy Ghost prayer. I didn't even know about the ones that *were* available. It was just Jesus and me as I began to learn how to walk with God.

As I mentioned earlier, I set aside time every single morning to meet the Lord in a certain place in my home. I did that every day for three years, and I count those three years as one of the most wonderful seasons of my life. I don't have words to tell you of all God did in my life during those three years. But every morning when I came to our special place, He was already there, waiting to enjoy sweet fellowship with me.

Dividing Our Lives Into Compartments

I loved that place of prayer so much that I almost went too far in my pursuit of it. I developed the attitude, "I don't want to do anything but be with Jesus." Everything else in my life became a burden. I'd perform all the routine activities of life, such as sleep, eat, and take care of my family and my home. But I did it all reluctantly, almost apologizing to God for what I considered to be a waste of time.

Jesus was so good to me in my ignorance. Over time, He taught me that one of the greatest hindrances to walking with God is the common practice of dividing our lives into two areas—the spiritual and the natural, or the sacred and the secular. One always seems to contradict the other.

I see this mistake being made all the time in the body of Christ. And I have to admit—I still make that mistake myself at times. But then I always go back to the revelation the Lord gave me during those three special years of growing in Him.

He showed me that I had divided my life into those two compartments of the spiritual and the natural. Each compartment had its own set of actions. Within my spiritual life were prayer, reading the Bible, worshiping God, and going to church. According to my worldview, this compartment of my life gave me great satisfaction and inner assurance and was well pleasing to God.

In sharp contrast to my perception of my spiritual life was how I viewed my so-called natural life, which encompassed such mundane activities as washing the dishes, grocery shopping, and cleaning the house. I was bored with this compartment of my life and was sorry I had to deal with it.

Because I divided my life this way, I was constantly feeling torn between the two. I lived in a constant state of "dis-ease," or uneasiness, always telling myself, *One day I'm going to lay aside this world. Then I won't have to waste my time with all these natural things that zap my strength!* It is as if I were walking an invisible tight rope between the two realms, finding no peace in either realm. What a misconception to be trapped in!

In Him We Live

How did I escape such a dilemma? I looked to Jesus, who is always our example.

Jesus knew no divided life. He lived in the presence of God from the time He was a small child until His death on the cross. God accepted Jesus' total life. The Father made no distinction between one act of Jesus and another. For instance, He made no distinction between Jesus' act of helping His earthly father, Joseph, in his carpenter shop and His act of raising Lazarus from the dead. We know that both acts pleased the Father because Jesus said, "I *always* do the things that please my Father." (John 8:29)

Paul gave us the exact same principle to live by in 1 Corinthians 10:31: "So then, whether you eat or drink, or whatever you may do, do all for the honor and glory of God." In other words, your entire life, your whole existence, should be a contribution to the glory of God.

Now, I'm not saying that every act we do is equal in importance to every other act. For instance, Paul sometimes sewed tents, and I'm certainly not saying that the times he sewed tents were equal in importance to the times he sat down to write his epistles to the churches. However, both of these acts were accepted and approved by God.

Acts 17 tells us about the time Paul visited the city of Athens. While there, he began to preach about the unknown God to all those within hearing distance. Then in verse 28, he made this statement: "For in Him we live and move, and have our being."

No part of your life is outside of God. If you are His child, then *in Him you live; in Him you move;* and *in Him you have your being.* You have one life, and that life is all in God.

In You He Lives

Now let's look at Psalm 139 to see another aspect of God's presence in our lives that's very interesting. Watch what David says here.

> O Lord, you have searched me [thoroughly] and have known me. You know my downsitting and my uprising; You understand my thought afar off. You sift and search out my path and my lying down, and You are acquainted with all

my ways. For there is not a word in my tongue [still unuttered], but, behold, O Lord, You know it altogether.

You have beset me and shut me in—behind and before, and You have laid Your hand upon me. Your [infinite] knowledge is too wonderful for me; it is high above me, I cannot reach it.

Where could I go from Your Spirit? Or where could I flee from Your presence. If I ascend up into heaven, You are there; if I make my bed in Sheol (the place of the dead), behold, You are there. If I take the wings of the morning or dwell in the uttermost parts of the sea, even there shall Your hand lead me, and Your right hand shall hold me.

PSALM 139:1-10

In this passage of Scripture, David suddenly has a dawning in his heart. He becomes aware of God's seeing presence. Then David receives a great but very simple revelation: the truth that *God is here*. There can be no place where He is not.

Now remember, David lived under the old covenant. So how much more as redeemed children of God can we say, "God is here"?

I could go ten million miles into space while you stay down here on earth, and I would truthfully be able to say to you, "God is here." At the same time, you'd be able to say to me, "Yes, and God is here too."

So this is what I found out about God in those first three years of Holy Ghost praying: *I don't have to go someplace to find Him.*

That's the whole message of the Gospel in a nutshell. The incredible truth of the new birth is that *God has come to me* through His Son, Jesus Christ. He has come to live inside me in the person of the Holy Spirit. And the greatest thing about being baptized in the Holy Ghost is not that I can speak in tongues, but that I can have the fullness of God Himself living within me, empowering me to walk with Him every day.

Aware of His Presence Within

The problem is, we don't live our lives with the continual awareness that God is living on the inside of us. We forget He is there! We're in much the same situation Jacob was in, in Genesis 28. Look at what happened to him.

> *And Jacob left Beersheba and went toward Haran. And he came to a certain place and stayed there overnight, because the sun was set. Taking one of the stones of the place, he put it under his head and lay down there to sleep.*
>
> *And he dreamed that there was a ladder set up on the earth, and the top of it reached to heaven; and the angels of God were ascending and descending on it! And behold, the Lord stood over and beside him and said....*
>
> GENESIS 28:10-13

Notice what it says in verse 13: "And behold...." In other words, it's saying, "Look! Don't you see?" The Lord was standing right there beside Jacob. In other words, He'd been there all the time!

> And behold, the Lord stood over and beside him and said, I am the Lord, the God of Abraham your father [forefather] and the God of Isaac; I will give to you and to your descendants the land on which you are lying.
>
> And behold, I am with you and will keep (watch over you with care, take notice of) you wherever you may go, and I will bring you back to this land; for I will not leave you until I have done all of which I have told you. And Jacob awoke from his sleep and he said, Surely the Lord is in this place and I did not know it.
>
> GENESIS 28:13,15,16

Jacob had the same problem we often have. The Lord had been with him all the time, but he wasn't aware of it. In other words, God's all-pervading presence was already there, and Jacob just unwittingly ran into Him! The world of the senses had intruded into his mind and captured all his attention.

As believers, we have an advantage over Jacob. The Holy Ghost doesn't just *walk beside us;* He *lives inside us.* And if we lived our lives with a continual awareness of the Holy Spirit's presence within us, we wouldn't do a lot of the stupid things we normally do!

Drawing Closer to God

This lack of awareness of God's presence goes back even further than Jacob. It goes all the way back to the first man, Adam. Adam was the first to walk intimately with God. But then he fell through disobedience, and everything changed for the worse.

However, the worst curse that came into the earth through the fall of man was that *the visible realm took over and became the enemy of the invisible realm.* Suddenly man's spiritual eyes were closed, and he couldn't see into the spiritual realm anymore. He died spiritually and his natural senses became dominant, consuming all his attention.

When we are born again, however, our spirits are once again made alive to God. The capacity to experience the spiritual realm is restored to us. Our spiritual eyes open, but like newborn babies, initially our vision is clouded. We don't see much.

That should change as we grow in the knowledge of the Lord. Our vision should get clearer as we continually draw near to God and develop our awareness of Him.

That's why God says, "Draw near to Me." He isn't telling us to come nearer to Him in actual distance; He wants us to draw nearer to Him *in experience.*

A father once talked to me about his son who had had problems in the past but had since gotten the victory. The father said, "I'm getting closer to my son every day."

I thought, *Closer? What do you mean, closer to him? He has lived in your house all the time. He has never left you.*

What was this father really saying? "I am getting closer to my son in *experience.*" Past barriers of conflicting feelings and thought patterns were breaking down, and a closer relationship was being built between father and son.

So it is in our relationship with the Lord. As we increase our awareness of His presence in our lives, the barriers of flesh come down, and we walk closer to Him every day.

Spiritual Receptivity

My husband and I have been pastoring for over twenty years. For a long time we noticed a common situation among Christians that bothered us. Then at one of our church staff meetings, we got into a discussion about this question: "Why is it that some Christians find God in a clear way and experience manifestations of His reality, whereas other believers seem to struggle along in their Christian walk, always looking for Him?"

So we discussed possible answers to that question. A few people said, "Well, you know, some people find God and experience His presence more because it's their personality. That's just the kind of people they are."

To be honest, I was a little bothered by that comment. So I went to the Bible to prove them wrong. I picked at random all sorts of people I considered to be great biblical characters who walked with God on a very high spiritual road. I intentionally picked people who were very different in personality, such as Abraham, Moses, Elijah, Isaiah, and Ezekiel.

Then I compared the lives and ministry of two more modern men of God who were totally different in personality: Charles Finney and John G. Lake.

All these men of God were totally and completely different from each other. They were different in education, in habits, in temperament, and in personality. Yet every one of them walked with God in a high degree of His glory.

So I sought the Lord about what all these godly men had in common. I asked Him, "What is it, Lord? If there's a common denominator, I want to know what it is! What is the vital quality that caused them all to walk so intimately with You?"

I believe the Lord gave me the answer in two words: *spiritual receptivity*. Spiritual receptivity is a quality in a person that keeps him open to heaven and constantly urges him "God-ward." For this person, spiritual awareness isn't enough. He goes on to cultivate that spiritual awareness until it becomes the greatest driving force in his life.

The spiritually receptive person differs from what we'd call "normal people" in this respect: When he senses an inward longing or yearning drawing him toward God, he immediately responds to it. He doesn't neglect the Holy Spirit's gentle tug in his heart. He doesn't allow distractions. When that longing comes, he does something about it. In doing so, he acquires a lifelong habit of spiritual response.

That's what each of us needs to do in our walk with God. The more time we spend in God's presence, the more we can increase our own spiritual receptivity.

You see, receptivity is the result of both *desire* and *response*. And I have found in my own life that receptivity is present by degrees. It can be increased by exercise, and it can be destroyed by neglect. It isn't a force that comes on you like a seizure. Receptivity is very gentle. It reminds me of a little seed. Once you plant that little seed in the ground, you have to water and protect it until it grows big enough to take care of itself.

It's the same thing with receptivity. You have to nurture and cultivate it by giving your attention to spiritual things like prayer and reading the Word. You have to protect it by keeping yourself from the hardening influences of sin and worldly passions.

Cultivate Your Awareness of Jesus

When Jesus died on Calvary, He died so every one of us could walk closely with Him. In Hosea 6:2, it says, "He will raise us up that we may live before Him." That doesn't mean we are to live before Him just when we are in our prayer closet. It means we are to live *all* our lives before Him. We are to walk with God moment by moment, continually aware of His abiding presence.

I'm endeavoring to broaden your understanding of what it means to walk with God. I want to help you throw off everything of the five-sense realm that attaches itself to you and draws your attention away from the invisible realm.

Hebrews 12:1 puts it this way:

> *Let us strip off and throw aside every encumbrance (unnecessary weight) and that sin which so readily (deftly and cleverly) clings to and entangles us, and let us run with patient endurance and stead and active persistence the appointed course of the race that is set before us.*

I also want to help you start cultivating a continual awareness of Jesus. I'm telling you, it will change you. It will change the way you walk. It will change the way you live.

You see, sometimes your spiritual eyes and ears can become dull and feeble from long disuse. But as you begin to set your gaze upon Jesus throughout the day, He touches you with His life-giving presence, and your spiritual eyes and ears come alive.

When the Lord began to teach me how to walk with Him, it certainly changed the way *I* lived. My new understanding delivered me from a constant state of frustration.

When you're in the ministry, things happen all the time to take you out of your prayer closet. Problems arise; people have needs; responsibilities must be fulfilled. You often don't get as much time alone with God as you'd like to have.

In fact, if I'd been in the ministry back during that special, three-year period with the Lord, I'd have been miserable. I would have fought constantly against myself and what had to be done.

But something happened within me that caused me to begin living my entire life as a contribution to the plan of God. I learned to just rest in the knowledge that in every area of my life—every day, all day long, no matter what I'm doing—I am contributing to God's glory in some way. I came to understand that as I live and walk before Him, my life is acceptable to Him, whether I'm eating, sleeping, fellowshiping with others, or spending time in prayer.

Do you know what the result of that knowledge was in my daily life? As I walked through my day, it released me to pray all the time instead of feeling as if I could only pray during a time of private devotions.

Praying Throughout the Day

You may ask me, "Sister Hammond, are you saying then that long, protracted periods of prayer are unnecessary?" No, I'm not saying that at all. I'm saying they are even more necessary than you may have imagined.

Those long periods of prayer lift your heart further into God. They enhance your gaze. They unveil further mysteries of God's kingdom. They enlarge your capacity to receive from Jesus. They enlarge your outlook so that as you walk, you can see Him more clearly.

I'm telling you, in my special place of devotions, there would be days when God's presence was so sweet,

I'd get up off my knees and say to the Lord, "Jesus, how will I ever leave You today? I cannot leave this place!"

Well, I learned that I don't have to leave Him. I just take Him right along with me all day long! As I began to walk with God this way, I prayed more than I ever prayed in the three years I kept a daily appointment with Him.

Now, granted, I do still have long periods of prayer. In fact, I have returned to my practice of giving my mornings to the Lord. But if I miss a morning, my life is in His hands and His presence still goes with me. I am always very aware of that presence, no matter what I do throughout the day.

So don't let the Devil trap you or put condemnation on you by saying, "You didn't pray enough today." Even if you pray three hours a day, the Devil will still tell you that you didn't pray enough when you get off your knees. Or you could pray in tongues for three hours, and when you're done, he'll say, "You didn't read your Bible today."

Satan will always try to make you feel like you haven't done enough. Don't let him do it. Through it all, just walk with God. Live according to the strength of the one "Who supplies you with His marvelous [Holy] Spirit and works powerfully and miraculously among you" (Galatians 3:5).

As you go through your day, the Holy Spirit will put different people or situations on your heart so you can make mention of them in your prayers. You may be driving in your car, taking a shower, or walking down the hall at the office when the Holy Ghost causes something to rise up in your heart. Whatever it is, just pray about it for a few moments. You'd be surprised to know how much God does through your simple prayers as you stay sensitive to Him throughout your day.

I can personally give many testimonies of times God has worked through me as I've made mention of particular individuals in prayer. I'm not talking about praying for someone for long periods of prayer, even though at times I do that as the Holy Spirit leads.

You know, some people expect the Holy Spirit to be like a stick of dynamite. They're looking for an explosion. They want the heavens to open and angels to come down and sing, "Pray about this"!

But the Holy Spirit isn't going to do that. More often than not, He will just put a person or a situation on your heart to pray about, and you'll pick up on His gentle nudge in your spirit.

At times someone comes to me and says, "Sister Hammond, I was thinking about you yesterday." I usually ask, "Well, did you pray when you thought about me?" I want people to realize that the Holy Spirit desires to use them in prayer as they walk in God's presence every day.

A Gulf War Miracle Through Prayer

Let me give you an example from my own prayer life of how the Holy Spirit operates. During the month of June before the Gulf War began, I began to pray for someone named Guy Hunter. I had no idea who Guy

Hunter was. I found out later that he was a Marine. He would also be the pilot of the first plane shot down in the Gulf War. But I didn't know that at the time. The Holy Spirit just gave me this unknown man's name and impressed me to pray for him.

The Holy Ghost will do that for you. He'll give you names of people you don't know. Now, you don't start off with experiences in prayer like that because if you did, your head would go "tilt." You wouldn't know what to do with that kind of supernatural information. But once you're more familiar with how the Holy Spirit operates, you'll begin to receive names of different people, places, and situations that your mind knows nothing about. That's when prayer becomes a marvelous adventure!

So I began to make mention of this man in my prayers. I never prayed long prayers over him. I never got on my knees to pray for him. But for three months, I'd lift him up in prayer as I walked through my day.

Then one morning I was listening to the news about the war and heard that the first pilot from America had been shot down. That night they released his name—Guy Hunter! When I heard that name, I shouted praises to the Lord because I knew Guy would be fine. I knew he was in the hands of God and that God would protect him and bring him home safely. I was so happy in my heart.

Well, that's exactly what happened. Guy was released from captivity, and he did come home.

About four years later, someone sent me a newspaper article about Guy Hunter because she had heard my testimony about praying for him. This article revealed the miraculous provision of God, who does superabundantly above all we could ever ask or think. (Ephesians 3:20)

The article was entitled "Retired Marine Recovers Wallet." In the article, Guy Hunter related that when he was shot down and the enemy was approaching him to take him captive, he buried his wallet in the sand because he didn't want them to find out his family's name or any other information about them.

Four years later, someone found Guy's wallet in the desert and sent it to him, perfectly intact! All the money and family photos were still there. Everything was just as it was when he buried the wallet four years earlier.

That's just one of hundreds of miracles that has occurred since I began to walk with God and stay continually aware of the Holy Spirit's leading in prayer. And I'm no special case. The truth is, miracles happen all the time when believers learn to walk in God's presence on a daily basis.

A New Level in God Each Day

As I said before, every day of your life, God wants to bring you to a new level in Him. It is His intention to make you equal to whatever natural situation you will face that day. He already knows your future, and He knows exactly how to prepare you to overcome every problem and obstacle that lies in the path ahead of you. This is the Gospel of the Lord Jesus Christ. This is what Jesus died for.

However, you have to take the time to get in God's presence so He can infuse you with His strength and bring you to that new level in Him.

So often that is where we miss it. We don't commune with God long enough for Him to touch our hearts with His presence. We pray a little prayer and then say, "Well, God, that's all for now. I have to go, so I'll see you tomorrow!" Then we push and strain in our own strength just to get through the day!

So I want to show you what *I* do each morning in my time with the Lord so He can bring me to a new level in Him and prepare me for the rest of the day. Perhaps what I share here will make it easier for you to let the Lord minister to you during your times with Him. Then He can get you ready to walk above anything that might be coming your way.

First, I always begin with the Word. (For this example, I'll use Psalm 84.) I usually have soft worship music playing in the background as I read the Bible out loud.

I begin reading: "How lovely are Your tabernacles, O Lord of hosts! *My soul yearns...*" (vv. 1,2).

As I read that phrase, "my soul yearns," the Lord touches me. I sense His presence on that phrase, so I stay there and say it over and over again as long as I sense His presence lifting me: "My soul yearns, Lord. My soul yearns for You. I long after You, Jesus." I can sense myself being lifted into a place in God that will help me walk out something in the natural that day.

Now, if I leave the phrase "my soul yearns" while it's still stirring my heart and I begin reading on, I won't reach the fullness of that new level in the Spirit to which God is endeavoring to bring me. But once that phrase stops moving me, I can go back and read a little more: "My soul yearns, yes, even pines and is homesick for the courts of the Lord; *my heart and my flesh cry out...*" (v. 2).

There is that gentle quickening of the Holy Spirit again. The presence of the Lord is touching the phrase "my heart and my flesh cry out." So I stay there and speak forth that phrase to the Lord: "My heart and my flesh cry out, Lord. My heart and my flesh cry out. *All* of me cries out for You, Jesus." As long as those words are touching my heart, I stay there. They are living words, and they are lifting me into the presence of God.

I just keep doing this, worshiping God with His own words of truth and life as the Holy Spirit leads. Soon an entire hour has gone by, but it has seemed like five minutes! I've been enjoying the presence of God. And it doesn't matter what comes my way that day—I am totally prepared!

No Shortcuts to God's Highest

Right now God is calling you to draw nearer to Him. If you are going to have the faith to do the things He wants you to do in this hour, you will have to obey that divine call.

It's a sobering thought to realize that God is going to hold you accountable for the things you know. He wants Jesus to shine forth from your life and win many for His kingdom. He wants you to be worthy of His call on your life. But how can you be worthy of that call if you aren't doing the most basic things He requires, such as spending time with Him daily in the Word and in prayer?

Jesus has already given you everything you need to walk in His highest and best in this life. He has made a way for you to approach God through His blood. He has healed you and delivered you. But the only way you can walk in that powerful deliverance in Christ is to live in union and in fellowship with the Father. There are no shortcuts; there is no other way.

That means it's time to set aside some time to take spiritual inventory of yourself! You need to get totally honest with God. He knows how much time you've been spending with Him, so don't hide from Him. Just say, "Father, I'm here for You to speak to me."

Then open the Bible and begin to read it prayerfully, keeping your spiritual eyes and ears open to discern what God is trying to say to you. You might find that some of the interests, activities, or relationships that you thought were the most important in the whole world are the very things the Holy Spirit tells you, "Just lay that down. It's hindering your walk with Me."

As you wait before God in His presence, find out how hungry you are for more of Him. Ask yourself how aware you are of His presence as you go through each day. Is God truly real to you? If He isn't, then you are backslidden—plain and simple. That doesn't mean you go out drinking, smoking, cursing, and committing adultery. It just means you were once walking with God and, at some point, you stepped back.

During this time of spiritual inventory, you will be certain to find room for improvement. None of us ever reaches a place in our spiritual walk where we can't go higher in Him.

But, thank God, you *can* be transformed to fulfill His good plan for your life. God has provided His grace and His power to change and equip you to do His will.

How can you find the divine grace and power you need to overcome every challenge that lies ahead? By choosing the "good portion"—walking continually renewed in His presence!

Prayer of Consecration

Perhaps there was a time in your life when you flowed wonderfully in the plan of God and knew what it was to experience His presence in your life. But then you moved away from God, and you don't sense His presence the way you once did. You are out of fellowship with the Father, and you know you need to jump back in.

Or you may be walking with God to a certain extent, but you've allowed your Christian walk to stagnate. You aren't as hungry for the things of God as you know you should be.

Whatever your situation, you can pray this prayer of consecration right now and recommit your life to Jesus. You can dedicate yourself not only to Him, but to the wonderful plan and destiny God has for you!

I seek You, Lord Jesus. You are everything to me. You have all the answers I need to every problem I face. In You is everything I need to finish my course with joy.

Forgive me for playing games with You. Please deliver me from complacency, and make Yourself real to me. Help me become so established and rooted in You that I stand tall and persevere over every attack of the enemy.

Father, I also seek to know You in a greater way. I cannot live without Your presence. Cause me to so hunger for You, Your Word, and Your power that I am never satisfied. Make my heart soft and pliable. Cause me to yearn and long for You. Fill me again with Your Spirit. Be nearer to me and dearer to me than I've ever experienced before.

Father, only You can meet the very deepest desires of my total nature. So I ask You to quicken me with Your presence. Help me lay hold of more eternal life. I know, Father, that it's a progression. I know that from this day forward, I will move upward until that day when I come and bow before Your throne.

Lord, I know that hungering after You is the only way I will have all of You. It's the only way I will wake up and arise to be a part of that spiritual army You are calling forth in this day.

What an awesome call that is, Father. To think that You want to use me, that You want Your glory to shine through me. What an awesome

Prayer of Consecration

responsibility! Please help me to always walk worthy of what You have called me to do.

So thank You, Father, for trusting me. Thank You for changing me into what You want me to be and for making me into the image of Your Son. In Jesus' name, amen.

Prayer of Salvation

A born-again, committed relationship with God is the key to a victorious life. Jesus, the Son of God, laid down His life and rose again so that we could spend eternity with Him in heaven and experience His absolute best on earth. The Bible says, "For God so loved the world, that he gave his only begotten Son, that whosoever believeth in him should not perish, but have everlasting life" (John 3:16).

It is the will of God that everyone receive eternal salvation. The way to receive this salvation is to call upon the name of Jesus and confess Him as your Lord. The Bible says, "That if thou shalt confess with thy mouth the Lord Jesus, and shalt believe in thine heart that God hath raised him from the dead, thou shalt be saved. For whosoever shall call upon the name of the Lord shall be saved" (Romans 10:9,13).

Jesus has given salvation, healing, and countless benefits to all who call upon His name. These benefits can be yours if you receive Him into your heart by praying this prayer:

Heavenly Father, I come to You admitting that I am a sinner. Right now, I choose to turn away from sin, and I ask You to cleanse me of all unrighteousness. I believe that Your Son, Jesus, died on the cross to take away my sins. I also believe that He rose again from the dead so that I may be justified and made righteous through faith in Him. I call upon the name of Jesus Christ to be the Savior and Lord of my life. Jesus, I choose to follow You, and I ask that You fill me with the power of the Holy Spirit. I declare right now that I am a born again child of God. I am free from sin and full of the righteousness of God. I am saved in Jesus' name, amen.

If you have just received Jesus Christ as your Savior, or if this book has changed your life, we would like to hear from you. Please write us at:

Mac Hammond Ministries
P.O. Box 29469
Minneapolis, Minnesota 55429-2946

You can also visit us on the web at
mac-hammond.org

About the Author

 **Lynne Hammond** is an internationally known teacher and author on the subject of prayer. Her books include *Heaven's Power for the Harvest, Staying Faith, When It's Time for a Miracle, Living in God's Presence, Secrets to Powerful Prayer, When Healing Doesn't Come Easily, Dare to Be Free,* and *The Master Is Calling.*

She is a frequent speaker at national prayer conferences and meetings around the country. Lynne also writes regular articles on the subject of prayer in the *Winner's Way* magazine and publishes a newsletter called *PrayerNotes* for people of prayer.

Lynne and her husband, Mac, are pastors of Living Word Christian Center, a large and growing church in Minneapolis, Minnesota. Under Lynne's leadership, the prayer ministry at Living Word has become an internationally recognized model for developing effective pray-ers in the local church.

The desire of Lynne's heart is to impart the spirit of prayer to churches and nations throughout the world.

Other Books Available From

BY LYNNE HAMMOND

The Master Is Calling
Discovering the Wonders of Spirit-Led Prayer

When It's Time for a Miracle
The Hour of Impossible Breakthroughs Is Now!

Staying Faith
How to Stand Until the Answer Arrives

Heaven's Power for the Harvest
Be Part of God's End-Time Spiritual Outpouring

Living in God's Presence
Receive Joy, Peace, and Direction in the Secret Place of Prayer

When Healing Doesn't Come Easily

Secrets to Powerful Prayer
Discovering the Languages of the Heart

Dare to Be Free!

The Table of Blessing
Recipes From the Family and Friends of Living Word Christian Center

Other Books Available From

BY MAC HAMMOND

Angels at Your Service
Releasing the Power of Heaven's Host

Doorways to Deception
How Deception Comes, How It Destroys, and How You Can Avoid It

Heirs Together
Solving the Mystery of a Satisfying Marriage

The Last Millennium
A Revealing Look at the Remarkable Days Ahead and How You Can Live Them to the Fullest

Living Safely in a Dangerous World
Keys to Abiding in the Secret Place

Plugged In and Prospering
How to Find and Fill Your God-Ordained Place in the Local Church

Positioned for Promotion
How to Increase Your Influence and Capacity to Lead

Real Faith Never Fails
Detecting (and Correcting) Four Common Faith Mistakes

Simplifying Your Life
Divine Insights to Uncomplicated Living

The Way of the Winner
Running the Race to Victory

BY MAC HAMMOND (CONTINUED)

Water, Wind & Fire
Understanding the New Birth and the Baptism of the Holy Spirit

Water, Wind & Fire—The Next Steps
Developing Your New Relationship With God

Who God Is Not
Exploding the Myths About His Nature and His Ways

Winning Your World
Becoming the Bold Soul Winner God Created You to Be

Winning In Your Finances
How to Walk God's Pathway to Prosperity

Yielded and Bold
How to Understand and Flow With the Move of God's Spirit

BY MAC AND LYNNE HAMMOND

Keys to Compatibility
Opening the Door to a Marvelous Marriage

For more information or a complete catalog of teaching CDs and other materials, please write:

Mac Hammond Ministries
P.O. Box 29469
Minneapolis, MN 55429-2946

mac-hammond.org